BRITISH AIRWAYS

AN ILLUSTRATED HISTORY

Paul Jarvis

In association with **BRITISH AIRWAYS**

AMBERLEY

First published 2014

Amberley Publishing
The Hill, Stroud
Gloucestershire, GL5 4EP

www.amberley-books.com

Copyright © Paul Jarvis & British Airways, 2014

The right of Paul Jarvis & British Airways to be identified as the Author of this work
has been asserted in accordance with the Copyrights, Designs and Patents Act 1988.

ISBN 978 1 4456 1850 0 (paperback)
ISBN 978 1 4456 1869 2 (ebook)

British Library Cataloguing in Publication Data.
A catalogue record for this book is available from the British Library.

Typesetting by Amberley Publishing.
Printed in the UK.

CONTENTS

FOREWORD

British Airways has the richest history in world aviation. I say that not out of chauvinism but out of honest reflection on the contribution to global transport made by my airline as we know it today and its forerunner companies.

Barely a decade and a half after the dawn of commercial flying in Europe, Britain's Imperial Airways had an unparalleled route network that stretched to southern and eastern Africa, the Middle East, India, Hong Kong and Australia. Journeys that would previously have taken several weeks could be accomplished in a few days.

Post-war, the story of expansion and innovation continued. Imperial had evolved into three new nationalised companies, BEA (for flights within Europe), BSAA (for South America and the Caribbean) and BOAC (for the rest of the world). Regular services across the Atlantic, to the Far East and all points in between became the norm. In 1952, BOAC started the world's first scheduled jet service, flying an aircraft that cruised at 500 mph – comparable with today's airliners and far faster than its predecessors. Flying times tumbled and the world started to shrink.

In 1958, BOAC beat the combined might of the American carriers to operate the first jet service between London and New York. When the jumbo jet started the era of mass long-haul travel, BOAC was quick to grasp its potential and large orders followed.

Forty years ago this year, BOAC and BEA were formally brought together as British Airways. With nearly 200 destinations in 88 countries, it had the most extensive route network in the world. Another aviation first soon ensued with the launch of supersonic travel. Though Concorde retired a decade ago, its iconic image lives on around the globe as a lasting symbol of British Airways' innovation.

That pioneering tradition has gone on, finding different forms of expression as times change. Privatisation, fully flat beds, online check-in, environmental performance – British Airways is proud of its record as an industry leader right up to the present day.

That is part of the culture that underpins our motto, 'To Fly. To Serve'. Those words were painted on our early aircraft and are emblazoned on our fuselages today. Whoever we are, our history is always part of us. The history of British Airways is indeed rich, and there is no better demonstration of that fact than this fascinating book.

Keith Williams,
Executive Chairman, British Airways

ACKNOWLEDGEMENTS

The opportunity to write this book was only possible due to British Airways' recognition of the value of its archive both as a corporate and national collection of importance. It is the airline's rich history of knowledge and experience that makes British Airways unique, reflecting nearly ninety-five years of commercial aviation history. That the archive exists and thrives is due to British Airways' continuing financial support and its willingness to allow me to manage and curate what we call the Heritage Collection. I thank them for that.

Figuring out how to reflect that rich history in a relatively short book was both a challenge and a pleasure, and an impossible task without the support of the Heritage Collection's volunteers. Their knowledge and experience underpins the support the archive provides to British Airways' business, and they are vital in welcoming visitors and guests to the Speedbird Centre that houses the Collection at the company's headquarters building near Heathrow Airport.

Particular thanks go to Jim Davies, who himself underpins my role in managing the archive and without whose support, suggestions and diligent proofreading this book could not have been written. Christine Quick's patience and skill in producing the large number of images required also warrants a special mention and thanks. We all also pay homage to the knowledge and experience of Keith Hayward, the archive's doyen volunteer, who, as a young British South American Airways traffic trainee, witnessed the very first flight to leave the then new London (Heathrow) Airport on 1 January 1946; Keith is a mine of information and anecdotes. My only regret is that the advice and guidance of Keith and others cannot be given justice in this slim volume. It suggests another edition in due course!

Paul Jarvis
British Airways Heritage Collection

British airways
the new name
in aviation

1

THE NEW NAME IN AVIATION

On 1 April 1974, the new name in aviation was British Airways. Formed from the integration of the UK's two nationalised airlines, BOAC (British Overseas Airways Corporation) and BEA (British European Airways), the new company advertised it had the world's longest and most comprehensive route network and biggest aircraft fleet operating international passenger, cargo and mail services.

In fact, British Airways was offering many more things: a world lead in airline computing and communications networks, associated company interests such as hotels, and technical services such as operating airports. With airline services as diverse as international long-haul wide-body jets, air charter helicopters and Highlands and Islands essential services, being almost all things to all men would be a tough act to develop successfully.

More than 200 Aircraft, Mostly Jets

The graphic opposite clearly captures the new British Airways' size and the diversity of its aircraft fleet. It also highlights British Airways' need to get to grips quickly with the complexity of its operations if it was to be the success it was set up to be. With twelve aircraft types, from the supersonic Concorde to helicopters, and with as many different engine types again, in engineering terms alone such a diverse operation would be a major exercise to manage efficiently, profitably and, above all, safely – the number-one consideration for the new company.

MORE THAN 200 AIRCRAFT, MOSTLY JETS

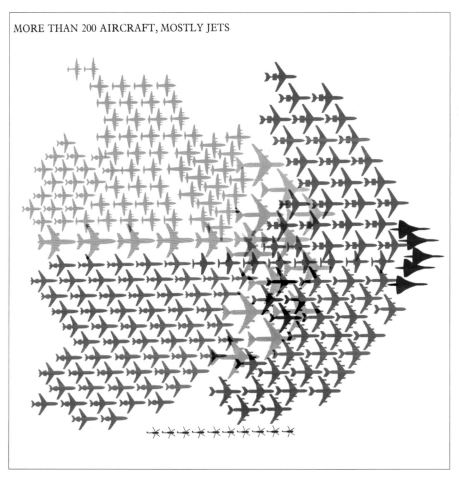

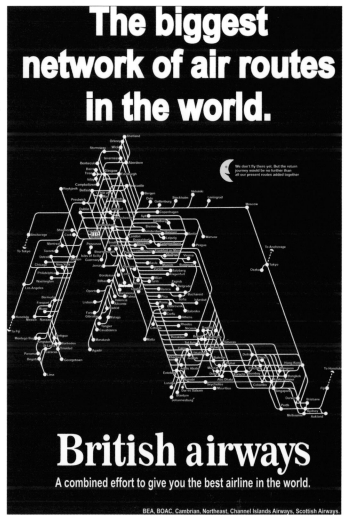

Right: The combined route networks of the airlines that made up the new British Airways gave the opportunity to claim it had the longest and most comprehensive route network in the world.

A New Image

British Airways had been born into a changing aviation world and those changes had been the force driving its formation. In the early 1970s the UK Conservative government was keen to promote competition in air services and in January 1973 had led the UK into the EEC (now the European Union). While there was as yet no EEC air transport policy and the old system of restrictive bilateral government agreements still applied, the UK Civil Aviation Authority was encouraging new entrants and lower airfares. Together with a growing drive in the USA to deregulate aviation markets, the cloak of protection for European national airlines began slowly to be removed. The thin veil of difference between scheduled and charter air services was as good as removed or ignored on many routes out of the UK, particularly on the North Atlantic, and competition between airlines further intensified. Airline industry agreements that fixed fares and standards of service also began to fail. While governments still controlled access to routes and approved fares and cargo rates, a greater freedom to innovate began to appear.

In the UK, the government actively supported the concept of a 'second force' airline and encouraged the private airline British Caledonian, giving it preference on several routes over BOAC. What had been a virtual state monopoly for BOAC and BEA for many years could not continue. The foundations were being laid for the bringing together of the two companies, 'integration' being a preferred term to 'merger', bearing in mind the strong emotions and sensitivities of the thousands of fiercely loyal BOAC and BEA staff, many of whom did not support the idea and believed it unnecessary.

From 1972 to 1974, the operations of BOAC and BEA were put under the control of a UK statutory body called the British Airways Board. The BAB oversaw a complicated arrangement of joint study groups and committees looking at all aspects of how the new airline might use its collective resources and how it would operate when launched. Not least was the issue of what the new airline identity might be; what would it look like and what should it represent?

In July 1973 a new British Airways image was launched. This predated the 'new name in aviation' launch by some ten months and was intended to provide time for the names of BOAC and BEA to be gradually phased out so that loyal customers – and the goodwill and brand recognition built up over the previous thirty years – would, hopefully, be retained and transferred to the new airline.

Henry Marking, later Sir Henry Marking, the BAB Group Managing Director, called the livery 'a symbol to be proud of'. As the former Chairman of BEA he could be expected to be pleased. Many thought the dominant tail fin design strikingly reminiscent of the old BEA 'quarter Union Flag' livery and the white-and-dark-blue fuselage and Speedbird symbol on each aircraft merely a nod to BOAC.

The design of a new livery for a company that was entirely new yet already one of the largest airlines in the world was a particular dilemma for British Airways' first design consultants, Negus & Negus. They needed to promote a new name in markets accustomed to the names BOAC and BEA and retain their business. It was also seen as important to encourage loyalty to the new company among the former staff of BOAC and BEA, who a short time before had been sometimes unfriendly and unhelpful rivals. Staff loyalty was believed to be so important that a comprehensive programme of staff consultations was undertaken before the final design was accepted. Elements of both the BOAC and BEA liveries were incorporated so effectively that many staff read the new livery as being an extension of the one they had previously served under, in spite of the final design having been arrived at by a completely objective route. Overall, the new livery was well received and perceived as modern, fresh and very suited to the British flag carrier, although it was criticised for being too 'American'.

Right: British
Airways sent
roadshows around
the UK to advertise
its new livery, this
one in Cardiff. The
tail fin flag design
by Dick Negus
was captured by
him in 1975 as
the centrepiece of
this painting that
now hangs in the
British Airways
Speedbird Centre
at its corporate
headquarters at
Harmondsworth,
near London's
Heathrow Airport.
(Dick Negus)

Far right: The
Boeing 747 provided
a perfect canvas to
advertise British
Airways' new livery.
The massive white
fuselage and huge
tail fin with the
quarter Union Flag
left no one in doubt
that this was Great
Britain's national
airline.

British
airways

26 September-25 October 1974
British Airways' new identification
comes to Cardiff
at The Design Council's Showroom
Pearl Assurance House
Greyfriars Road, Cardiff

Open Mon to Fri 09.30 to 17.30
Admission Free

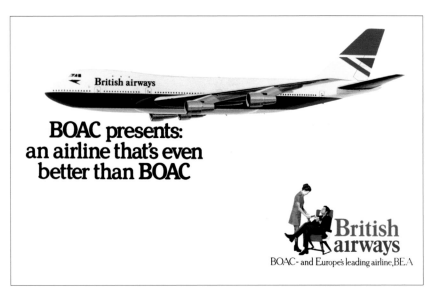

**BOAC presents:
an airline that's even
better than BOAC**

British
airways

BOAC- and Europe's leading airline, BEA

**The best of BOAC and BEA combine
to take even better care of you.**

The mantle of BOAC has been taken
over by a new and great name in the sky.
British Airways.
And the traditional care and attention
to the individual needs of air travellers
throughout the world will continue with
even greater courtesy and efficiency.
Incorporating the former British
European Airways (BEA) - itself the
No. 1 European carrier, with an unrivalled
network of European services - British
Airways is the largest international
airline in the world.

We fly to almost 200 destinations in
84 countries, with all the services and
facilities only a great organization can
offer. To vacationers, to visiting friends
and relatives from any country; to
businessmen; to people of all ages from
all countries.
When we say British Airways is the
best of BOAC and BEA to take even
better care of you, we mean it.

British
airways

Now there's an airline that can fly you to
more places than any other airline. Nearly 200
cities; in Britain, in continental Europe, in 88
countries all over the world.
      Now there's an airline with more aircraft
flying internationally than any other airline.
      Now there's a worldwide airline with
people who are famous for the care and the
efficient service they give wherever you go.
      Now whether you're flying on business,
on holiday or visiting friends, there's an airline
you can rely on to put your well-being first.
      Now the world is yours.

British airways
The best of BEA and BOAC

Above left: During 1972 and 1973, both BOAC and BEA continued to advertise using their old names and at the same time promoted the new name, British Airways. This was designed as a gradual phasing-out process to encourage the transfer of brand loyalty to the new company prior to the dissolution of BOAC and BEA on 31 March 1974. (Foote, Cone & Belding, now Draftfcb London Ltd)

Above right: In long-haul overseas markets a greater emphasis was placed on the key feature of the new airline's livery, the quarter Union Flag tail fin, to emphasise its 'Britishness' as well as spell out its links to its predecessors. BOAC's successful brand strapline had been 'We'll take good care of you'; British Airways capitalised on its success by continuing to use it but with added emphasis: 'We'll take even better care of you'. (Foote, Cone & Belding, now Draftfcb London Ltd)

Left: British Airways' UK launch campaign highlighted the airline's new livery and linked it back to its predecessors as 'The best of BEA and BOAC'. (Foote, Cone & Belding, now Draftfcb London Ltd)

The Armorial Bearings of British Airways

THE NEW NAME IN AVIATION 11

ARMS (shield)	Argent between a Chief and a Bendlet sinister couped Gules, a Gyron issuing from the dexter, the point in sinister chief Azure.
CREST	On a Wreath of the Colours, rising from an Astral Crown Or, a Sun irradiated proper.
SUPPORTERS	On the Dexter a Pegasus Argent crined, unguled and winged Or, gorged with an Astral Crown Azure, holding in the mouth a sprig of Olive fructed proper; on the Sinister, a Lion guardant winged at the shoulders Or and gorged with an Astral Crown Azure. The whole upon a compartment of a grassy mound proper dimidiating water barry wavy Azure and Argent.
MOTTO	TO FLY, TO SERVE

To Fly. To Serve

Both BOAC and BEA had coats of arms designed by the English College of Heralds, BOAC's in 1941, a year after it was formed, and BEA's in 1946. Formally known as 'armorial bearings' but often referred to as 'coats of arms', they were important parts of each airline's image and livery. In a traditional heraldic sense they identified each airline and those associated with them. BOAC's was almost royal in its depiction of lions supporting a heraldic shield, but BEA's was rather more 'knightly', being a simple shield and a motto, '*Clavis Europae*', or 'Key to Europe'.

In 1975, the British Airways Board was granted a coat of arms and a motto – 'To Fly. To Serve' – and this was also used by British Airways. It was similar to BOAC's, not from any leaning towards its predecessor but because its make-up represented a much wider operation across the world. Simply put, on the new battlefield that international commercial aviation was to become in the final decades of the twentieth century, British Airways and its new livery would stand out and its motto, 'To Fly. To Serve', would be the standard around which its staff and loyal customers would rally. Almost forty years later, British Airways would reaffirm its commitment to its motto with a renewed and strengthened emphasis on what it does and who it is.

While heraldry is clearly symbolic it is also practical, even in the twenty-first century. As a corporate device it is often widely used as part of a company's instantly recognisable branding. The heraldic language used to describe a coat of arms may be from a bygone age but it does represent in heraldic terms what British Airways was established to do, and its motto is a reflection of its commitment to customer service, both then and now.

British Airways' coat of arms includes a central shield that shows the family origins of the bearer; this is a quarter Union Flag, as at the time it was the UK's national (state) airline. The shield is supported by a winged horse and winged lion. A lion is the heraldic symbol for England and is shown with wings to reflect flying and a crown to reflect supremacy. Above the shield is the helm, or helmet, turned to the right to signify a company in public ownership and topped by an astral crown and a full sun.

Above left: BOAC and BEA issued a joint advertisement in 1953 to coincide with the coronation of HM Queen Elizabeth II. The advertisement was carried in the coronation issue of the UK's *Sphere* magazine and highlighted both companies' coats of arms as 'symbols of all that is best in air travel' and a hint at their established place in the best of British tradition.

Above right: BEA's coat of arms comprised a shield with a helmet and bird (a swift) to denote its relationship to aviation as a nationalised (state) airline and speed. Its motto was '*Clavis Europae*' ('Key to Europe'), a motto that was widely used by BEA in its early years to promote its services as exactly that, i.e. the key to travel to Europe. The shield was widely used and carried both inside and outside BEA's aircraft. The company's initials were often shown as part of the shield's red banding, although this was not strictly part of the original coat of arms.

Opposite: Together – BEA, Cambrian, Channel Island Airways, Northeast, BOAC and Scottish Airways stewardesses. Six airlines made up the new British Airways, four making up the Regional Division with BOAC as Overseas Division and BEA as European Division. One first step towards integration was the adoption of the BEA uniform, by the British designer Sir Hardy Amies, as the first British Airways uniform. Made of heavy, worsted wool material, it was not ideal for long-haul operations to hotter climates and the BOAC summer uniform in coral pink and Caribbean blue, by the British designer Clive Evans, was retained for those routes.

Engineering a Merger

Engineering a Merger is an account of engineering management and staff participation in the amalgamation of the engineering departments of BOAC and BEA following the formation of British Airways in 1974. It sets out the complexities and sensitivities facing both sides in reaching a solution to the differences in working practices and sometimes arcane agreements established since civil aviation recommenced following the end of the Second World War in 1945. Its background was writ large across the two companies. Each operated quite different route networks. BEA's aircraft were referred to as 'coming home at night' to be maintained, whereas BOAC's might be seven operational days away on the other side of the world. While both companies were in the air travel business, the infrastructure to maintain such different operations made integration a complex and difficult task.

Compounding the operational issues was the forced continuation of BOAC, BEA and the regional airlines such as Cambrian as separate operating divisions of British Airways. In effect, for the first two years the airline was being run as three separate businesses, hardly an incentive to unite, and with a duplication or even triplication of many services and costs across them. Against the background of the world's fuel crisis of the early 1970s and a tripling of aviation fuel costs, plus severe industrial unrest as the various trades unions fought their corners, British Airways struggled to reap the benefits of the integration.

On the commercial side, while the respective passenger sales and advertising departments of BOAC and BEA were brought together quite quickly – as early as 1973 – under a new British Airways Travel Division (BATL), its executive management reported through to a joint Board of Control. The board was run by the three autonomous airline divisions that decided on BATL's UK commercial policy, but BATL did not control overseas selling, which was left to the airline divisions abroad. In effect, there were managers everywhere and a long chain of command.

Management Services ran a slicker operation and integrated more quickly and effectively, but in supporting BATL and overseas selling they had to contend with two entirely different computerised sales systems, BOAC's 'BOADICEA' and BEA's 'BEACON', which had to be integrated and staff retrained – major tasks that had to be completed quickly.

With the benefit of hindsight it is easy to be critical and oversimplify the issues and answers facing British Airways as it struggled to unite. By any measure it was a mammoth task and all undertaken during a major worldwide economic downturn. Being a nationalised airline, British Airways was still subject to the diktats of government policy, from funding approval for aircraft purchase to imposed fuel quotas, all limiting management's ability to make the best and most effective decisions on its many and complex divisional activities. That British Airways improved its turnover by 20 per cent in the 1973/74 financial year and 15 per cent in 1974/75 was no mean feat, though severe industrial unrest almost wiped out any profit in the latter and manpower levels remained high, a serious Achilles' heel for management.

Above left: Engineering a Merger identified even the locations of the separate BOAC and BEA engineering bases at Heathrow Airport as a serious hurdle to overcome. The public road that divided the two bases was considered to represent a 'psychological barrier' that encouraged the various management and staff study groups to continue to think in terms of the old organisations. Even after the contentious divisional organisations had been abolished in 1977, the road was considered to 'continue to exert a prejudicial influence upon any plans for integration'. This overhead photograph of Heathrow in the early 1970s shows the two bases, BEA's to the left and BOAC's to the right, and the contentious road marked in red.

Above right: BEA's 'BEACON' reservations centre at its West London Air Terminal. The serried rows of BEACON terminals look almost like toy-town machines today and the many staff not unlike those in a call centre, which in a way it was; a far cry from booking seats today via the internet.

Looking Ahead

One particular asset that British Airways had inherited was its predecessors' pioneering spirit. Despite the trials and tribulations of its formative years, the new management took early decisions on the essential matter of fleet replacement and the need to continue to innovate in order to give itself a fighting chance of success. BOAC had received its first three Boeing 747 aircraft, with Pratt & Whitney JT9 engines, in May and June 1970, and six more in January 1971; its wide-body fleet stood at seventeen by 1975 and allowed British Airways to withdraw from service its Boeing 707-436 aircraft and the standard Vickers VC10. The 747 fleet would be further augmented in 1977 with another four, but this time with Rolls-Royce RB211-524 engines.

The RB211 family of engines would set a standard in the future British Airways' fleet as it sought to reduce its dependency on a variety of engine types and old aircraft inherited from its predecessors. BEA had led the way in 1972, ordering six Lockheed TriStar-1 aircraft powered by Rolls-Royce RB211-22B engines to replace its Hawker Siddeley Tridents. The TriStar fleet was also planned to increase to fifteen by 1982, plus a possible long-range version, also with the RB211-524 engine that powered the 747s.

A major new UK promotional campaign, with the theme 'Fly the Flag', was launched in June 1975 to build on the success of the original launch of the British Airways name and branding, which by then was becoming well established. The central theme was to encourage travel abroad across all British Airways' markets and segments, from businessmen to leisure and VFR (visiting friends and relatives). A key visual was the quarter Union Flag tail fin central to British Airways' new livery and the simplified strapline, 'We'll take more care of you.' With a range of new products, particularly in the leisure market, such as 'Sovereign' and 'Enterprise' holidays, the new campaign was to become British Airways' first major UK advertising launch in its own name and around a unifying national theme – the Union Flag and the promotion of British success.

The TriStar-1 was the first large jet aircraft to be used by British Airways on the former BEA European routes. When the aircraft were originally ordered by BEA they were intended for the Mediterranean mass-package holiday routes as a replacement for their Trident aircraft. However, by the time the aircraft were delivered the integration with BOAC had taken place and the package holiday market had changed. The aircraft were too large for most of the European capital city routes and did not have the range for the majority of long-haul routes. The aircraft were eventually used on routes such as Paris that just about warranted an aircraft of almost 400-seat capacity at peak times and on some UK–Gulf services, but they struggled to operate with full loads in the heat of the Gulf summer.

TriStar Superflights to Paris, Brussels and Madrid

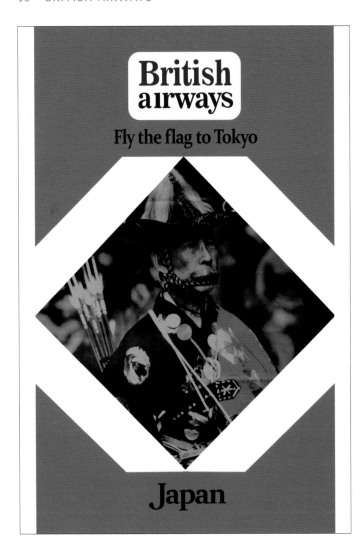

British airways

Fly the flag to Tokyo

Japan

Left: One of a set of British Airways' first destination posters under the 'Fly the Flag' advertising campaign, this one for Japan.

Right: An early success for British Airways was the introduction a shuttle service between London and Glasgow on 12 January 1975. A first for Europe, the concept was borrowed from the successful Eastern Airlines New York to Washington shuttle and was an instant success, despite the early misgivings of some. Passengers just turned up at the airport, were guaranteed a seat and payment was made on board by cash or cheque. To fulfil the guarantee, standby aircraft and crews were on hand and would fly a back-up aircraft, even for only one passenger. The shuttle concept of a very frequent, flexible service continued for many years and was successfully extended from London to Edinburgh, Belfast and Manchester, although not to Europe. In later years, on-board payments were discontinued as they were expensive and difficult to administer; confirmed seat reservations then became the norm and back-up aircraft were no longer used. (Foote, Cone & Belding, now Draftfcb London Ltd)

Shuttle
Shuttle
Shuttle
Shuttle
Shuttle
Shuttle

Repeat after us.
If I'm going to London from Jan 12th, I don't need to book.
All I have to do is turn up at Glasgow airport any time up to the hour, any hour from 8 in the morning till noon or from 2 till 8 at night any weekend, (every 2 hours-8.00a.m. to 8.00p.m. at weekends), and there'll be a jet waiting for me.
I can get my ticket in advance from my British Airways Travel Agent or pay on the plane.
Either way I'm guaranteed, repeat guaranteed, a seat.
It's easy coming back, too.
Shuttle. Just turn up and take off.
It's as simple as that.

British airways

We'll take more care of you.

Have a Superflight through Africa.

Holiday stopovers from $203.

British Airways offers you two exciting Speedbird holidays on your way to London or the USA.

Nairobi: A marvellous opportunity to experience the wildlife adventure of a Safari Holiday in one of East Africa's most exciting Game Parks. Inclusive 3-day stay from only $238.

Seychelles: Spend three glorious days in these beautiful islands for only $203 inclusive.

For further information contact your local Travel Agent or British Airways, International Building, Orchard Road. Phone 371422.

Superflight by **British airways**

We'll take more care of you.

Above: Collecting the cash: an early shuttle flight operating the 'pay on board' system.

Left: 'Have a Superflight' was a sub-brand of the 'Fly the Flag' campaign. Roz Hanby, a British Airways stewardess and their new publicity girl, became a very well-known part of their advertising from the mid-1970s to 1980s. (Foote, Cone & Belding, now Draftfcb London Ltd)

... and Looking Back

From a single route to nearly 200 destinations worldwide, British Airways claimed to have the longest and most comprehensive route network in the world; that single route over which the world's first commercial scheduled service operated in August 1919, between London and Paris, had taken around two and a half hours, sometimes three or more, depending on the weather. Nearly sixty years later, Concorde would fly the 3,500 miles between London and New York in a little over three and a half hours. That great leap forward took years of hard work and innovation, a collective spirit that took centre stage in the British Airways 2011 TV advertisement *Aviators*, which looked inside what made the company what it is today, and how it all began.

In 1919 a British airline had the largest system of International Air Routes.

Strange how history repeats itself.

Hounslow, Middlesex

Le Bourget, Seine

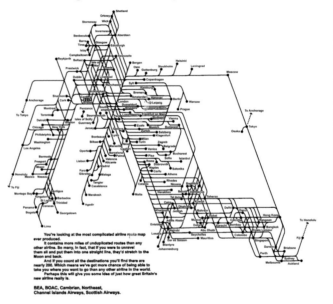

You're looking at the most complicated airline route map ever produced.

It contains more miles of unduplicated routes than any other airline. So many, in fact, that if you were to unravel them all and put them into one straight line, they'd stretch to the Moon and back.

And if you count all the destinations you'll find there are nearly 200. Which means we've got more chance of being able to take you where you want to go than any other airline in the world.

Perhaps this will give you some idea of just how great Britain's new airline really is.

BEA, BOAC, Cambrian, Northeast, Channel Islands Airways, Scottish Airways.

In 1974, British Airways took its own look back to link its past with its future. A then-and-now comparison, but such a simple approach could not do justice to the breadth and depth of British Airways' history, although it makes an interesting comparative advertisement. (Foote, Cone & Belding, now Draftfcb London Ltd)

2

HOW IT ALL BEGAN

In the opening scene of *Aviators*, a very small aircraft sits in a field surrounded by rather a lot of people, some taking photographs or waving. Whether it was quite like that we'll never know, but it sets the scene perfectly for a story of endeavour, innovation and sheer hard work, not quite a *Boy's Own* tale but close in the early years. What we do know is that those first services were nothing like today's travel experience. Operating from an often muddy airfield and taking up to three very noisy hours or more to fly from London to Paris, the journey was not exactly something to look forward to, but those early travellers often did and some of their experiences are legend. At least those early aircraft and their pilots, often of First World War vintage, were quite used to occasional forced landings in a convenient field to pump fuel by hand or fighting the elements before a safe arrival at their destination. One account reports that, after a very bumpy flight over the Channel fighting the controls of his aircraft, the pilot was very concerned to enquire after the health of his passengers; to his surprise they very much enjoyed the experience and thanked him for putting on a good show of aerobatics for their benefit!

The world's first commercial scheduled passenger service took place on 25 August 1919 between what was then London's only commercial airport at Hounslow Heath, just 2 miles or so to the south-east of today's Heathrow, and Paris (Le Bourget). Hounslow Heath was a military airfield licensed for commercial flying and that first air service was operated by a small private company called Aircraft Transport & Travel, a predecessor airline of British Airways. Using various converted First World War military aircraft, AT&T would go bankrupt by the end of 1920, unable to operate in what had became a free-for-all among fledgling UK and foreign airlines fighting for market share.

While traffic volumes were low in these very early days, air travel had captured the public imagination, helped by the considerable publicity given to it in the media. In early September 1919, *Sphere* magazine carried an enthusiastic report of the journey made by one of their reporters on an AT&T flight to Paris. The *Sphere* reporter was actually their artist and made copious sketches during the journey, which the magazine printed in full, predicting that air travel was here to stay and 'marking the beginning of a new era in illustrative journalism'. What had impressed the artist and the magazine's editor was the ease and comfort of the journey, which allowed sketches and writing to be carried out 'as easily as on *terra firma*', often difficult in a bumpy train or a rolling ship, and in half the time. For the businessman particularly, let alone leisure travellers, air travel was the new way to go.

In 1979, to commemorate its sixtieth anniversary, British Airways commissioned the artist Terence Cuneo to paint a picture of the first commercial flight of AT&T. The picture now hangs at the entrance to the British Airways Speedbird Centre at its corporate headquarters at Harmondsworth, near London's Heathrow Airport. (Terence Cuneo)

Above left: Almost the reverse view of Cuneo's painting, an AT&T flight to Paris gets ready for departure. What is surprising by today's standards of safety and security is the almost casual interest and participation of all manner of different people, from airfield employees to the general public, but these were early days.

Above right: *Sphere*'s artist, Mr Davis (left), has his travel documents checked by an official (Mr Phelps, Chief Customs Officer for Hounslow Heath) before taking off for Paris on 3 September.

Below left and right: Some agility was required to get into the AT&T de Havilland DH.16s, but at least normal clothing was satisfactory, provided the sliding windows were kept closed! Conversely, the first service to Amsterdam in September 1919 (a charter flight), in a de Havilland 9B, required somewhat warmer wear as two female passengers joined the pilot in a 'cabin' open to the weather.

The London–Paris Air Express

There are few accounts of the very early days of air travel that might be considered accurate, but *The Romance of a Modern Airway*, written in 1930 by Harry Harper, is as near as one can get. Harper was a friend of Sir Sefton Brancker KCB, AFC, then the UK Director of Civil Aviation, who wrote the foreword to his book and reminded us that Harper was one of a select group of people trusted by the UK government to educate the public in 'the tremendous possibilities of flying and the great influence that it must inevitably bring to bear on the future of the British Empire'. Such foresight did not extend, however, to any financial support to the fledgling industry and the London–Paris route became a battleground between UK and French aviators that only a year or so before had been allies, although in very different circumstances.

The UK airlines – AT&T, Handley Page and Instone – tried to compete but on very unequal terms; the French airlines were subsidised by their government and whether by foresight or not it allowed them to undercut the British and make inroads into what market there was. While the British aircraft and overall product offerings were broadly comparable to those of the French, without a subsidy the British airlines could not cover their costs, let alone make a profit.

A Handley Page evaluation made in January 1920 on the economics of operating the London–Paris route estimated that if they could operate their proposed thrice-weekly ten-seat round-trip service at a one-way fare of 15 guineas (£15.75), with a consistent 60 per cent load factor (unlikely) and achieve 90 per cent service reliability (very unlikely), they could break even. Such fares were also around the level of a first-class combined rail and sea journey, so although the air journey made a considerable saving in time – the 'air express' unique selling point – it was insufficiently attractive in itself to encourage a mass market at those prices. Although most airlines were only operating small aircraft of up to ten seats and the total route capacity was not high, it was still a lot to fill on a daily basis and high load factors were very unlikely to be achieved. The *Sphere*'s artist reporter had been charged £42 for his round-trip journey. Despite the accompanying media hype about the advantages of flying, the public would take a lot of persuading at those prices to start queuing up, and so it proved.

AT&T struggled and was taken over by the Birmingham Small Arms Company, who kept it operating until December 1920. Handley Page then stopped operating the London–Paris route altogether, followed by Instone in early 1921; by February there were no British airlines operating the route until a temporary British government subsidy was introduced that allowed the two airlines to start up again. Fares had to be slashed to match the French and by the following year a more permanent subsidy was applied based on payment by results. In effect, the British government underwrote 50 per cent of the cost of the aircraft used and 25 per cent of gross earnings, plus £3 per passenger. By 1922, when a new British airline, The Daimler Airway, entered the fray, fares across all airlines had standardised at £6.60 one way and £12 round trip. The result was more passengers, and loads increased to the extent several services were often full, but it could not last. Given the high inflation and unemployment of the early 1920s, the government struggled to balance its books; the temporary subsidy was as good as an open chequebook and there was no real control on how it was spent and little idea of its effectiveness. Flying would become a mode of transport for the rich and famous and not, for many years, for the man in the street. The fledgling industry would need to adapt to the need for comfort, even luxury, as well as safety, reliability and good overall service, if it was to survive.

An Instone Air Line de Havilland 34 flying over Croydon around 1922/23. This particular aircraft became part of Imperial Airways' original fleet in 1924 and, although only having a single engine, was operated by them until 1926 when new, multi-engine aircraft were delivered. (Kenneth A. McDonough)

Royal Mail contracts were critical to the British airlines' survival. The Post Office had quickly recognised the potential for using air services to speed mail deliveries and mail carriage was considered more important than carrying passengers; a Daimler Airway DH.34 aircraft is loaded at Croydon in 1923.

Left: Services to other Western European countries quickly followed the Paris start-up. Daimler Airway inaugurated the first London–Berlin flight in September 1922; Daimler's Managing Director Col Frank Searle and General Manager G. E. Woods Humphery pose for a photograph prior to the departure of the return leg from Berlin.

Right: As well as supporting a good cause, Instone Air Line would receive some much-needed publicity for its services. An Instone DH.34 at Croydon is bedecked with the rose flower motif of the (Queen) Alexandra Rose Hospital Charity Day on 13 June 1923, the last time it was held.

LONDON-PARIS AIR SERVICE

Daimler HIRE Lᵀᴰ.

FINEST MOTOR CARS *for* CITY SERVICE *or* TOURING THROUGH EUROPE

DAIMLER HIRE LIMITED.

By Appointment.

THE DAIMLER AIRWAY

MANCHESTER
LONDON
AMSTERDAM

Above: The Daimler Airway's first Paris service was an all-cargo operation carrying newspapers and was heavily overloaded. The pilot only just managed to glide his DH.34 into Le Bourget, having run out of fuel in flight. Early air services were sometimes operated on the edge of what would now be considered completely unacceptable standards, but these were pioneer days and the aviators were trying hard to prove they offered a viable new mode of transport.

Far left: Daimler Hire's 1922 brochure gives equal prominence to its car and air services. The Daimler Airway was formed as a subsidiary of Daimler Hire as early as 1919 but did not start London–Paris services until 2 April 1922; it ceased operating to Paris only six months later, due to fierce competition between British and French airlines.

Left: Daimler Hire's 1923 airline brochure only shows services to Amsterdam, although Paris is mentioned inside in conjunction with Handley Page Transport; an early example of co-operation between British airlines trying to compete against subsidised French companies.

Comfort in the Air

By 1922, when the first *ABC Air Guide* was published, there was a remarkable degree of sophistication in the airline services on offer, no doubt prompted by the need to cater for the wealthy customers' expectations and to provide a degree of differentiation in products, given all the airlines were charging the same fare. Instone advertised their services as 'the last word in safety, luxury and comfort', with well-ventilated cabins, sliding triplex windows and upholstered armchairs; they also emphasised that special clothing was not necessary and motor cars would meet the 'machines' on their arrival at both ends of the route. Instone staff, even office staff, all wore uniforms and may have been the first airline staff to do so. Instone clearly appreciated the need for high standards in their product presentation, probably learnt from their extensive experience in the shipping industry. 'Machine' was also a common reference term for aircraft. The 1920s marked the beginning of the so-called 'machine age', which implied modernity and advancement, a cornerstone of a new world order, and the airline business was quick to exploit that link.

Daimler used its experience in the car-hire business to launch its own airline, The Daimler Airway, as an extension of that business. With a fleet of 250 limousines and chauffeurs to do the airport delivery and pick-ups, Daimler advertised its aircraft as 'Air Liners' and 'truly liners of the air', with cabins as 'miniature replicas of the luxurious saloons of the ocean liners' providing every convenience, including heating, a steward and refreshments – and, of course, a lavatory; early passengers had been sometimes inconvenienced by a lack of lavatories and by 1922 most airlines offered them.

References to 'comfort' were a recurring theme in these early years. Given that the combined train and sea journey remained a major competing product for the nearer cross-Channel cities of Paris and Amsterdam, passengers needed to be persuaded that to fly was not only safe but comfortable and enjoyable as well as fast.

As well as most of the amenities offered by the other airlines, Handley Page had edited and printed for its passengers a *London Weekly Diary of Social Events*, listing the principal events of each week's London social calendar – everything from theatres to sporting events that their wealthy passengers might be interested in. It was possibly the first example of a premium giveaway.

Above and opposite: The Paris Aviation Exhibition of 19 December 1919 was a major showcase for British aircraft manufacturers and airlines. Handley Page exhibited a complete W.8 aircraft, G-EAPJ, painted white, presumably to make it stand out as white was not its usual livery. Handley Page was unusual in that they both manufactured and commercially operated their aircraft. The W.8 was an early civilian design and, unlike earlier Handley Page aircraft, was not a converted First World War bomber.

The interior of G-EAPJ was rather plush for such an early aircraft and was no doubt decked out especially well for the exhibition.

Right: The Handley Page 0/400 was a converted First World War bomber with a gun turret in the nose that could be converted into a passenger seat just in front of the pilots. It was an early version of what became known in later years as 'flying in the jump seat' in an aircraft's cockpit, a treat that security measures now strictly forbid. It must also have been a rather nerve-racking experience, especially on landing.

HANDLEY PAGE TYPE 0/700.
(Interior)

Above left: The customer experience was very much of opposite extremes in the early days of air travel. While every attention was given to comfort on the ground, once passengers reached the aircraft the experience became rather more basic. A mechanic's set of steps made for ease of access to the aircraft cabin, although not without some risk or loss of dignity.

Above right: The Daimler Airway's first arrival at Gothenburg in the early 1920s. Daimler was the first airline to use uniformed stewards on board their aircraft, seen second left in the photograph. Stewards were often recruited from the airlines' competitors, the railways and shipping companies; stewards with high levels of customer service experience were needed if the airlines were to compete for the same clientèle.

Opposite left: The interior of a Handley Page 0/7 aircraft. One class of service was the norm in these very early days, with aircraft weight and structural design limitations governing what passenger comforts could be provided. Lightweight cane seats complement more homely creature comforts such as curtains, flower vases and a mantle clock to time the journey – everyday things to encourage passengers to be at ease. A map of the air route would often be pinned to the aircraft's cabin ceiling as an early version of today's 'moving map'.

Opposite right: A Handley Page 1922 advertisement emphasising the safety features and on-board comforts of flying in their W.8 'machine', the same white-painted aircraft exhibited at the 1919 Paris Exhibition. The airfare included free motor car travel from the airline's booking offices in London and Paris to the airfields, a service expected by the often wealthy passengers; every airline offered it as a matter of course.

Those Brave Young Men

The early pilots were considered a breed apart. Most had First World War experience and many hours of flying, often in difficult conditions, operating the flimsy and unreliable aircraft of the time. With few navigational aids and very rudimentary wireless communications, they were no longer gladiators of the air but certainly heroic in the eyes of many. Unreliability, particularly of aircraft engines, was a real risk in the early days of flying. Handley Page was the first to specify using twin-engine aircraft for safety reasons and advertised that their 'machines' could 'travel for many miles on only one engine'. Safety was then and remains now the number-one airline priority, but the risk profile was very much higher at the beginning of the twentieth century than at the beginning of the twenty-first.

Much less heroic, but quietly effective, was the role of the aircraft engineer. By today's standards, the aircraft engine was a rather basic in-line or rotary piston engine driving a propeller, but it was a marvel of the time and intricate beyond most people's imagination. Famous names such as Rolls-Royce, Bristol and Napier engines powered many British aircraft and the men that understood and maintained these laboured away unseen in sheds more reminiscent of backstreet garages.

The early airframes were even more basic, a collection of canvas and wire and wooden struts that easily broke. To put that all together and make it fly was a valuable skill but a scarce resource; the huge loss of young men in the carnage of the First World War meant that qualified and experienced engineers were in short supply. Despite performing many male civilian roles during the war, a woman's place was now back in the home and operating 'machines' was considered a man's occupation, both in the air and on the ground. Women would not even achieve full voting rights until 1928, and it would take several more decades and another world war before women could begin to take an active part in the operational side of civil aviation. By the mid-1920s, it was recognised that the availability of future pilots and engineers would need to be assured if aviation was to grow.

Flying was considered the new way to travel but it also had an image problem to overcome; the prospect of an air journey was exciting but not necessarily for those of a nervous disposition. This rather jolly image of two Handley Page pilots at the controls of one of their 'machines' was included in their 1922 brochure *By Air To Paris*. Meant to instil confidence in their experience and professionalism, and making them look rather like 1920s racing drivers, the truth was that these pilots were highly skilled and experienced, often honed from combat flying during the First World War.

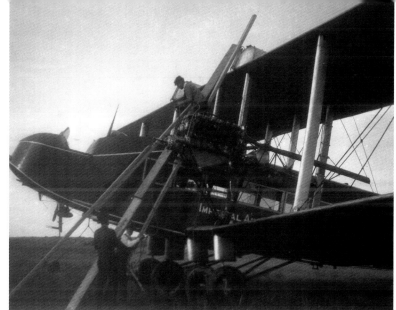

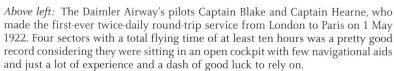

Above left: The Daimler Airway's pilots Captain Blake and Captain Hearne, who made the first-ever twice-daily round-trip service from London to Paris on 1 May 1922. Four sectors with a total flying time of at least ten hours was a pretty good record considering they were sitting in an open cockpit with few navigational aids and just a lot of experience and a dash of good luck to rely on.

Above right: By the standards of the twenty-first century it is amazing that ground engineers were able to carry out such major tasks as changing aircraft engines with nothing more than planks of wood and chains. It says everything about the skill and hard work that the ground engineers put into keeping these early aircraft flying in all weathers.

Below right: The Daimler Airway's engineers maintaining a Bristol 'Napier' engine from a DH.34 at their Croydon workshop. Such intricate and highly skilled work demonstrates the huge advances made in aero-engine technology in only twenty years, driven by necessity during the First World War.

Nationalisation

On 1 April 1924 the new name in aviation was Imperial Airways, an airline set up by the British government to develop air links with its overseas empire and with a name to match that grand ambition. At last the British government had not only recognised the importance of civil aviation but also that it needed to be supported both financially and preferentially if it was to succeed. The previous arrangement of financial subsidies had to end; subsidy alone could not guarantee that the interests of Britain and its empire would be best served nor the money well spent among competing commercial companies.

The British government was Imperial's principal shareholder, placing several directors on its board so that they could influence its activities and keep an eye on its expenditure. The remaining board members were selected from directors of the four previously subsidised airlines: Daimler Airway, Handley Page, Instone and British Marine (a very small company that operated wooden flying boats between the Channel Islands and Southampton). By Act of Parliament, in effect a forced takeover, the four airlines were bought by the government and merged to form the new company.

Imperial became Britain's first nationalised airline. The price for the restrictions imposed on Imperial by nationalisation – for example, having little freedom of choice in aircraft purchase, being forced to 'Buy British' – was countered by the protection and effective monopoly rights of being the favoured British airline, supported by the Treasury and the powerful and experienced Civil Service. No other major European government had taken this approach. It gave Imperial an advantage and an opportunity to tap into the extensive overseas resources of the British Foreign Office and Royal Air Force, both organisations already in place along many of the embryonic routes Imperial would need to pioneer in its task of establishing an Empire airway.

Almost the whole of the serviceable Imperial Airways' fleet in May 1924: three Handley Page W.8bs and three de Havilland DH.34s at Croydon.

THE FIRST AND ONLY PASSENGER TICKET

ISSUED AND USED FOR THE

FIRST FLIGHT MADE BY IMPERIAL AIRWAYS

26 APRIL 1924

DAIMLER HIRE LTD. AIRWAY
ROYAL DUTCH AIR SERVICE CO.

AIRWAY TICKET No. **LR.55522**

BY AIR **LONDON** TO **AMSTERDAM** RETURN
(or ROTTERDAM)

Name of Passenger *Major Beaumont*

Date of Passage *26-4-1924*

Service   Seat No.

Fare Paid   ..   £   :   s.   d.

Issued only subject to the Terms and
Conditions printed herein.

DAIMLER   HIRE, LTD.

By Appointment
243, KNIGHTSBRIDGE, LONDON.

Fifteen Aircraft, Mostly Obsolete

Imperial Airways was in a much worse fleet situation than British Airways in 1974. In taking over and nationalising the assets of Daimler Airway, Handley Page, Instone and British Marine, only fifteen usable aircraft formed the fleet of the new company. Many of the aircraft were single-engine and therefore effectively obsolete, as one of Imperial's first decisions was to adopt the same policy as Handley Page and plan to operate only multi-engine aircraft. This meant that in the first year of operations nine of the single-engine aircraft were scrapped and two crashed. It was an inauspicious start and a daunting one, given the huge task Imperial had to face to develop a route network of many thousands of miles over water, desert, mountain and other inhospitable terrain with a fleet of aircraft completely unsuited to the task.

An early decision was made to rebuild the fleet, but this would take another two years. Meanwhile, Imperial would have to make do with what it had and at least continue to operate the few European services previously served by its four predecessors. Paris was the main destination, with Amsterdam and Brussels close behind as intermediate points on the routes to Germany. Switzerland was served via Paris. At least bringing the assets and staff of its four predecessors together was much less difficult than for British Airways fifty years later, although a pilots' strike over pay and conditions delayed the beginning of Imperial's operations until 26 April 1924.

Due to a pilots' strike, Imperial Airways did not fly its first service until 26 April 1924, when it reportedly flew to Paris. Rather than waste the resources of its predecessor airlines, Imperial used old Daimler Airway ticket stock for its early passengers, this one marked as 'the first and only passenger ticket issued and used for the first flight made by Imperial Airways 26 April 1924' – but to Amsterdam?

Above left: By March 1926, just before new aircraft types joined the fleet, Imperial Airways had managed to reorganise its fleet to twin-engine types.

Above middle and right: A Supermarine Sea Eagle being launched at Southampton, one of two taken over from British Marine Air Navigation. The fuselage was made of mahogany and painted dark blue by Imperial Airways as part of its first livery. British Marine operated from Guernsey to Southampton, an overwater route for which the six-seat Sea Eagle was well suited. It certainly looked like a 'flying boat' with wings, tail and engine added. Captain Bailey also looks the part, rather like a deep-sea diver!

An Empire Airway

In 1926, Imperial took delivery of its first new aircraft. Importantly, these were designed as civil airliners and were not ex-military types. No longer would passengers have to sit in converted gun turrets or improvised interiors but in proper cabins with improved seating. Also importantly, the new aircraft had three engines, so reliability and performance improved – a major consideration for the overseas routes these airliners were intended to pioneer.

While Imperial had used its first two years to consolidate its European routes, it had also been planning how it would develop its Empire routes. North Africa, particularly Cairo, was seen as a hub from which, initially, routes to the Middle East and India would be operated, followed by Cape Town and West Africa; finally, Australia would be linked.

In December 1926, Imperial flew the first of its new aircraft, a de Havilland DH.66 Hercules, to Cairo as a positioning flight. The aircraft was to take over from the Royal Air Force the mail service between Cairo and Baghdad, known as the Desert Air Mail Service. Mail was a premium cargo in these early days of aviation, far more important from a revenue perspective than passengers and a major ingredient of Imperial's purpose to develop and speed up communications with the British Empire. Although the Desert Air Mail Service was not between Empire territories, the route passed over key sectors of the eventual route between Britain and India, the jewel in the Empire crown.

Also in December 1926, Imperial operated a demonstration flight from London (Croydon) to Delhi by extending the route from Baghdad around the northern end of the Gulf of Arabia beyond Basra and southwards along the Persian shore towards British Baluchistan and on to Karachi, then in India. The journey took twelve days, with Delhi a further two days away. The aircraft was one of the DH.66s and, on its arrival in Delhi, was named *City of Delhi* in honour of that city. The journey aroused intense media interest and was closely followed by the British and Indian public, being seen as a triumph of modern technology and British resolve. When regular services eventually started in March 1929, travelling by air to India in just seven days rather than several weeks by sea was seen as a marvel and a great adventure, albeit not without some discomfort from flying through, rather than over, the weather, but at least without any jet lag.

Imperial Airways' de Havilland DH.66 G-EBMX arrives in Delhi on 8 January 1927. The flight created enormous interest both in the UK and India and huge crowds greeted the aircraft. As well as creating the first air link between the two principal countries in the British Empire, it implied a bright future for a world still emerging from the terrible shadow of the First World War.

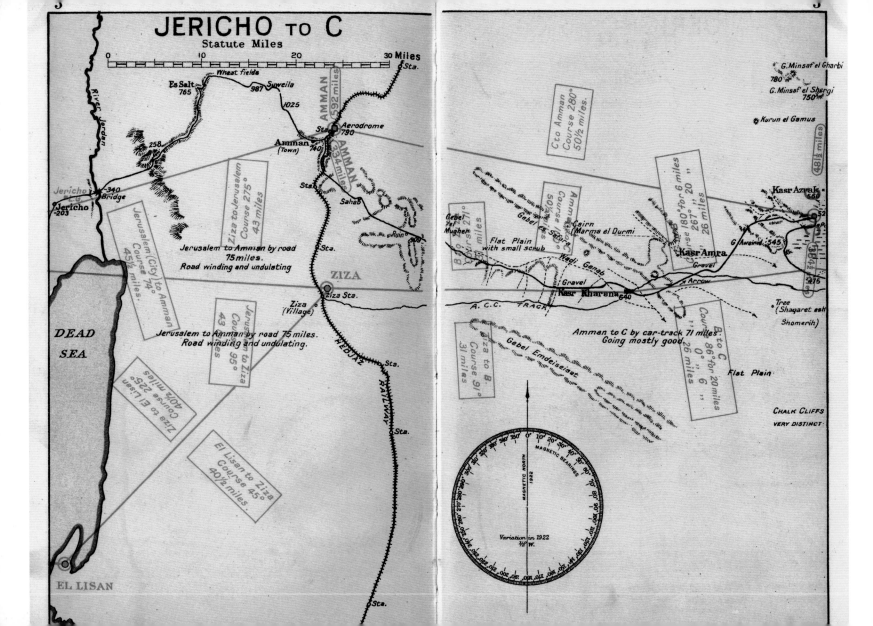

JERICHO TO C

Statute Miles

0   10   20   30 Miles

Es Salt
765

Wheat fields

Suweila
987
1025

AMMAN (592 miles)

Aerodrome
790

Amman
(Town)
740

258

AMMAN 334 miles

Jerusalem to Amman
Course 74°
45½ miles.

Ziza to Jerusalem
Course 275°
43 miles.

Jerusalem to Amman by road
75 miles.
Road winding and undulating

River Jordan

Jericho −340
L.G.
Bridge

Jericho
−203

Sta.

Sahab

Ruin

Sta.

ZIZA

Ziza Sta.

Ziza
(Village)

Jerusalem to Ziza
Course 95°
43

Jerusalem to Amman by road 75 miles.
Road winding and undulating.

DEAD SEA

Ziza to El Lisan
Course 225°
40½ miles

El Lisan to Ziza
Course 45°
40½ miles.

HEDJAZ RAILWAY

Sta.

Sta.

EL LISAN

Sta.

Sta.

G. Minsaf el Gharbi
780

G. Minsaf el Shergi
750

Kurun el Gamus

C to Amman
Course 280°
50½ miles.

481½ miles

Amman Course 50½ miles

Course 100° for 6 miles

26 miles "97°" "20"

B course 27° miles

Gebel Pef Mughet

Gebel es Safara

Cairn
(Marma el Durmi

Kasr Amra
Gravel

Kasr Azrak
560

G. Aweinid 545

Flat Plain
with small scrub

Wadi Genab

Gravel

Kasr Kharana
540

Arrow

A.C.C. TRACK

Ziza to B.
Course 91°
31 miles

Gebel Emdeiselaat

Amman to C by car-track 71 miles
Going mostly good

B. to C
Course 86° for 20 miles
" 0° " 6 "
" 26 miles

Flat Plain

Tree
(Shaqaret esh Shomerih)

CHALK CLIFFS
VERY DISTINCT

MAGNETIC NORTH
1922

MAGNETIC BEARINGS

Variation in 1922
½° W.

Above and right: One of Imperial Airways' new Armstrong Whitworth Argosys, G-EBLF, at Croydon in August 1926, prior to receiving its certificate of airworthiness. G-EBLF was used to start the 'Silver Wing' luxury air service to Paris eight months later, repainted all silver from its original dark blue. Its cabin seating started life as eighteen lightweight cane chairs but later changed to cloth and leather as the service was upgraded.

Opposite: A page from a Royal Air Force pilot handbook of 1925, showing a sector of the route of the Desert Air Mail Service. Imperial Airways' pilots used the handbook to guide them across a largely featureless desert between Cairo and Baghdad. Where landmarks were particularly sparse the RAF had ploughed a large furrow across the desert, marked as a black line on the map, to be used as a marker for pilots to follow. (HMSO)

The Silver Wing

Imperial Airways' second new aircraft was the Armstrong Whitworth Argosy. Delivered in June 1926, the aircraft went into service on the London–Paris route the following month. The route was then the busiest in the world, and the Argosy was a welcome addition to Imperial's old fleet. With eighteen seats and a larger passenger cabin than anything previously flown, comfort in the air began to become a reality; improved seat design and space gave the on-board steward the opportunity to provide a better standard of service and greater personal attention than before. In May 1927, Imperial launched its 'Silver Wing' service, considered the world's first luxury air service, using a combination of Argosy and older Handley Page W.8b aircraft. For one extra guinea (£1.05), passengers enjoyed a meal service and hot drinks plus a bar, although the meal service was rather rudimentary compared to later years, when full galleys could be installed. The Argosy flew the prime service, taking two and a half hours for the £9 one-way fare, and the W.8bs flew the secondary service, taking two hours and fifty minutes for a cheaper fare of £7.50. It was the first example of two-tier pricing and stole a march on Imperial's French competitor, Air Union, which had introduced its 'Golden Ray' service to match the 'Silver Wing'.

The 'Silver Wing' was a great success for Imperial Airways and continued up to September 1939 with various improvements, ultimately providing a five-course hot-and-cold luncheon and seven-course dinner, all served on fine china and glassware. In the mid- to late 1930s, while Imperial's fleet largely comprised aircraft of old design technology such as biplanes, their on-board standards and customer experience was second to none and highly respected.

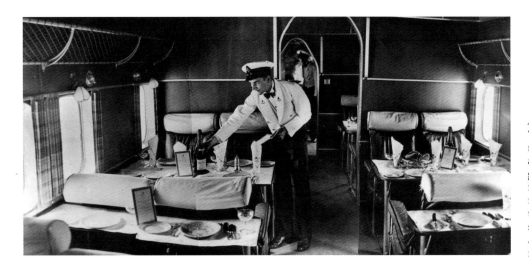

Above and opposite: The 'Silver Wing' service started as a 'service de luxe', but in name only, with drinks and light refreshments from a buffet trolley. By the 1930s, however, as newer and larger aircraft came into service with proper galleys, it was luxury indeed. Imperial Airways were the first airline in the world to provide full-course meals in flight, with seven-course dinners and five-course lunches on the London–Paris route in the 1930s. The image shows the steward 'laying the tables in the saloons of Imperial's liner *Scylla* in readiness for the next service', *Scylla* being the name given to one of its Short L.17 aircraft.

Above: Imperial Airways stewards not only served the meals but also had to collect them from the Croydon kitchens.

Right: By the 1930s, the 'Silver Wing' product had developed into a true luxury service, even on the original Armstrong Whitworth Argosy aircraft shown in this poster. The Argosys were supplemented in 1931 by the larger Handley Page HP.42 aircraft and, in 1934, by the Short L.17, both with proper galleys allowing five-course lunches and seven-course dinners to be served. (Charles C. Dickson)

Opposite: The Stankle sisters about to board an Imperial Airways flight to Paris in the summer of 1927. This was one of the first 'Silver Wing' services using the new Armstrong Whitworth Argosy aircraft.

Imperial Airways Invite You to See All This by Air

The 'Silver Wing' service was just one example of Imperial needing to differentiate its product from its competitors and appeal to its discerning clientèle. Promoting Imperial's services was another major activity that blossomed during the 1920s and 1930s. The creation of an art of the airways followed, with advertising posters, timetables and all manner of passenger ephemera, all wonderfully illustrated, the artists being given free rein to promote the new air services and encourage more people to travel. In reality, however, airfares were high and Imperial's main clientèle remained the wealthy, businessmen, government officials and the military travelling on duty. Expanding the travel base to the man in the street would take several more decades, although Imperial made several innovative attempts such as its promotion of 'Tea flights over London'. For £1.50 passengers could enjoy a short flight from Croydon Airport over the main London landmarks while being served tea and cakes. Concorde charters over the Bay of Biscay some sixty years later would provide a similar opportunity for those unable to afford the normal supersonic service.

Using many famous artists of the day, Imperial's advertising portfolio became a compendium of attractive artworks reflective of their time. 'Comfort in the air' was a recurring message, wrapped around almost idyllic images of immaculate service and luxury while aloft. For short distances in good weather that was often the case, but on longer journeys in more unstable climes journeys could be more arduous, with the only saving grace the considerable saving in time. It would take a lot of advertising to disguise that reality and changes in aircraft technology to overcome it.

Comfort in the air, 1931 style. The scene could almost be from a railway or shipping brochure, both modes of transport serious competitors even for short European journeys. Airline standards of service were a consideration for many wealthy short-haul passengers when deciding which way to travel. (Tom Purvis)

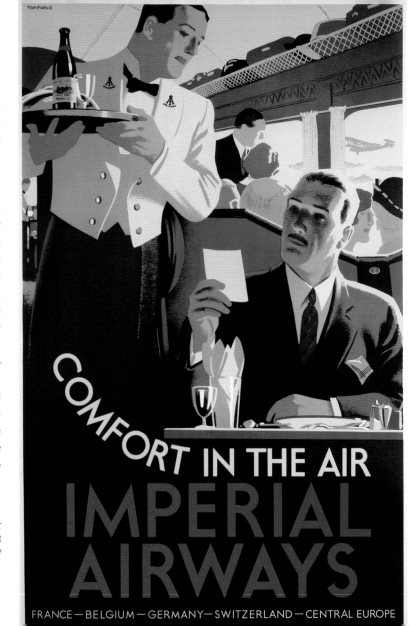

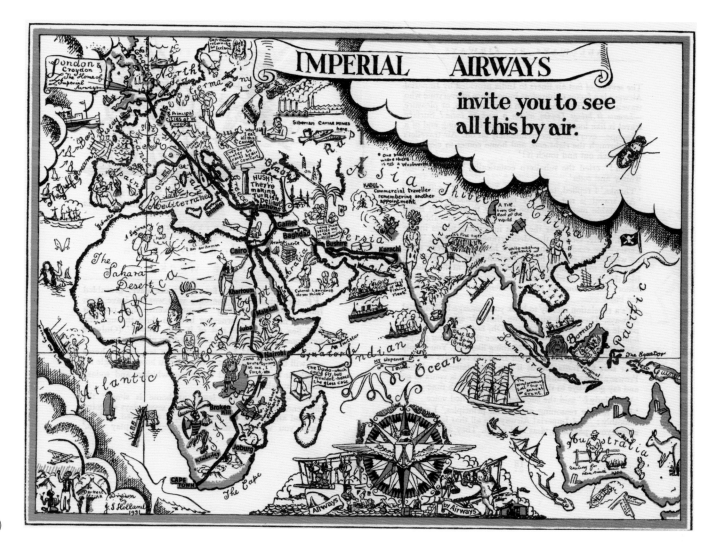

The centrefold map of an Imperial Airways brochure issued in the early 1930s, after the airline had inaugurated the principal Empire air routes; it was a tantalising and enticing image of what were then considered distant and mysterious places, known only from geography books. (J. S. Holland)

Far left: The 'Flying Chef' character created by Fougasse, the pen name for Kenneth Bird, for Imperial Airways has been resurrected by British Airways as a mark of impeccable service and attention to detail for its current First customers. (Kenneth Bird)

Left: Le Touquet, on the French coast just south of the main airway to Paris, was a popular gambling resort for the wealthy British in the 1920s and 1930s. Imperial Airways ran regular services to cater for the demand for weekend breaks at the casino.

Opposite: Tea in the air over London: an unthinkable pleasure today, but Imperial Airways' Argosy aircraft were often seen flying low over London's sights of interest in the 1920s and 1930s. (Theyre Lee-Elliott)

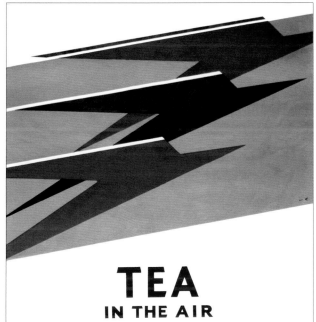

IMPERIAL AIRWAYS
COMFORT & CONVENIENCE

When travelling by Air in Europe

Welcome Aboard

It would take Imperial several more years to build a fully commercial aircraft fleet, but the gain would be short-lived as foreign aircraft manufacturers pushed the envelope of aircraft design ever further. By contrast, the British laboured with tried-and-tested designs such as larger and rather stately biplanes and flying boats. Imperial's restriction to 'buying British' meant it could not always meet its rivals on an equal technological footing, but it did have the advantage of a British monopoly on its Empire routes and the protection of government bilateral agreements controlling who could fly where and how often.

Stately biplanes and flying boats were, however, quite acceptable to Imperial's clientèle on the very long routes to far-flung outposts of Empire. Those routes were often many thousands of miles long over difficult terrain and, invariably, involved crossing seas or oceans. While slow and with a limited range, often able only to fly a few hundred miles before needing to refuel, Imperial's aircraft were surprisingly comfortable, with luxury fittings and saloon-like cabin interiors and even promenade decks on the later flying boats. On a 1931 journey to India, for example, the adventure, for that is what it surely was, began with a flight to Paris, then a rail journey to Brindisi in southern Italy; from there a flying boat to Athens and on to Haifa, then a change to another aircraft to Karachi via Baghdad. With six night stops, sometimes in tents by the seashore, and low-altitude flying with opening windows, the views must have been spectacular and exciting; to a travelling public of whom most were probably only broadly aware of such places from their school geography lessons, it was an adventure indeed.

The Handley Page HP.42 epitomised Imperial's 1930s fleet. It was large and slow, with a top speed of 105 miles per hour dependent on the strength of any headwind. It was also a biplane at a time when many competitors were changing to faster monoplane types, but what it lacked in speed and grace it compensated for through luxury cabins and low depreciation, with a relatively long life for aircraft of the time, operating into the early 1940s. With forward and aft saloons seating thirty-eight passengers on the short-haul European version and eighteen seats for long haul, it was considered a true air liner and a real match for the luxury trains and ships it competed with on European routes, let alone Imperial's airline competitors.

Right top: An Imperial Airways HP.42 somewhere en route to India, possibly at Gwadar in what was then British Baluchistan. The aircraft shown is named *Hanno* and was the first aircraft to operate the southern routing to India along the Arabian Gulf through Bahrain, Dubai and Sharjah in 1932.

Right bottom: HRH The Prince of Wales was a keen flyer and Imperial Airways had the honour, on 26 March 1929, of welcoming him aboard an Argosy aircraft on one of the early royal flights. In the decades to follow the royal family would patronise Imperial Airways and its successors as the airline of choice for both state and personal air travel.

Opposite: Comfort & convenience when travelling by air in Europe: an impossibly idyllic scene, but artistic licence allowed the inference which, in part, was true. By the late 1920s and early 1930s, air travel was certainly convenient over other transport modes and remarkably comfortable in good weather. (Rex Whistler)

Imperial Airways' fleet of Short S.8 Calcutta (three-engine) and Short S.17 Kent (four-engine) flying boats at their Alexandria base in the early 1930s. Imperial began operating the trans-Mediterranean sectors of its UK–India service in April 1929, using flying boats on the sectors between Italy, Greece and Egypt.

Right: The forward saloon of the HP.42 aircraft.

Far right: The New Road to The East, a promotional brochure designed for Imperial Airways to promote its new services to India. (Charles C. Dickson)

All Ways by Airways

All Ways by Airways is the title of a rather entertaining booklet produced in 1932 by Imperial Airways. With a series of cartoon characters, it sets out what passengers and shippers could expect when flying on Imperial Airways, from lunch in the air en route to Paris, Cape Town in eleven days or the more mundane aspects of airmail and sending goods by air. Airmail was hugely important to the airline. It was the mainstay of Imperial's turnover and critical to its profitability; while flying was still a novelty and unattainable to the 1930s man in the street, anyone could write a letter and send it by air. The prospective market was therefore huge and only limited by the cost of sending small consignments and the technology needed to increase uplift. The answer was the Empire Air Mail Scheme, and the Short 'C' Class flying boat.

The Empire Air Mail Scheme was an ambitious programme proposed by Imperial Airways and the Post Office to carry all first-class mail within the Empire by air. The idea was to encourage the volume of mail and to introduce more aircraft capacity to meet the expected demand; it was also hoped to encourage more passengers and increase the revenue contribution from what was, at this point, considered secondary traffic to airmail. A new aircraft was called for, which Imperial ordered 'off the drawing board' from the British manufacturer Short Brothers of Rochester. The Short 'C' Class flying boat was an obvious choice given the lack of airfields across most of the Empire routes and the many waterways such as the sea, rivers and lakes, where landing facilities could be quickly and easily provided. Imperial ordered twenty-eight 'boats' in 1935 and deliveries began in 1936; mail and passenger traffic quickly increased and 'C' Class operations expanded across the Empire. In 1939, following earlier trials, the first transatlantic all-mail services began between London and New York.

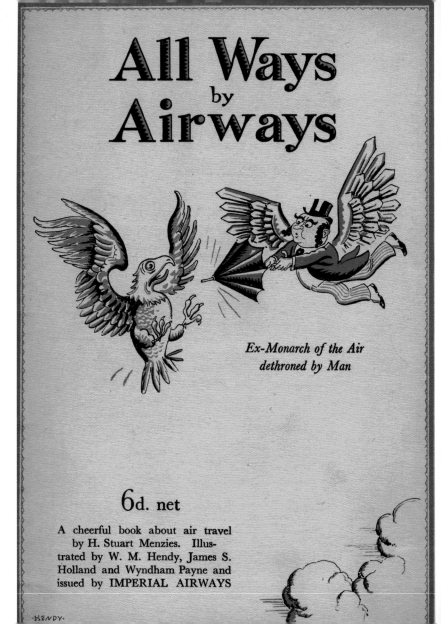

Ex-Monarch of the Air dethroned by Man

6d. net

A cheerful book about air travel by H. Stuart Menzies. Illustrated by W. M. Hendy, James S. Holland and Wyndham Payne and issued by IMPERIAL AIRWAYS

Above left: The first airmail to India was carried on 30 March 1929 by an Imperial Airways Argosy aircraft on the first sector – to Paris – of its seven-day journey. Mail services to South Africa and Australia followed over the next few years and on 26 May 1934 Imperial's service was recognised with the award of its first official airmail pennant from the UK Postmaster General, Sir Kingsley Wood. The pennant was carried on Imperial's HP.42 aircraft *Hengist* when it left for India later that day. The airmail pennant and the Union Flag were flown from Imperial's aircraft after landing and during taxiing, but pilots sometimes forgot to lower them before take-off – much to the detriment of the flags!

Above right: Imperial Airways' new Atalanta aircraft *Andromeda* arrives for the first time at Rand Airport, Johannesburg, in autumn 1932. Imperial had started the UK–South Africa route in June that year, a journey taking eleven days and with twenty-eight stops en route, including two days by train between Paris and Brindisi, Italy. The Atalanta took over the East Africa to South Africa sectors of the route in 1933.

Opposite: The front cover of Imperial Airways' customer booklet *All Ways by Airways*. (W. M. Hendy)

The most luxurious Flying-Boat in the world

Length 88ft. • Height from water line 24ft. • Speed 200 M.P.H. (Approx.)
Span 114ft. • Weight fully loaded nearly 18 tons • Crew 5 • Accommodation 24 passengers
in day stage and 18 in night passage

The Empire Flying-Boat—28 are now being built for

IMPERIAL AIRWAYS

Above: Delivering the 1938 Christmas mail to Coogee, New South Wales.

Right: Breakfast on board the Imperial Airways 'C' Class flying boat *Calpurnia*, late 1930s. (Robert E. Coates Photography)

Opposite: A cutaway of an Imperial Airways Short 'C' Class flying boat; although these aircraft had substantial accommodation for passengers, including cabins, lounges and a promenade deck, it was the mail that took priority.

Above: Imperial Airways' 'C' Class flying boat *Calypso* and Qantas Empire Airways' *Corio* at Imperial's 'Empire' base embarking dock, Berth 108, Southampton, late 1930s. (Qantas)

Left: A rather atmospheric image of the Imperial Airways 'C' Class flying boat *Calypso* being refuelled at Lake Habbaniyeh, near Baghdad, en route to India. (Robert E. Coates Photography)

The Second Force

While Imperial Airways had been concentrating on developing the Empire routes, some felt it had neglected its European operations. In particular, Scandinavia and Northern Europe had few services to speak of apart from Paris and points south en route to the Empire. The development of the Empire Air Mail Scheme was taking up much of Imperial's attention by the mid-1930s and, to be fair to them, they really had little choice. With few suitable aircraft for purely European operations, Imperial's fleet largely comprised long-haul types best suited to developing the Empire routes, which is what they had been set up to do. The European version of the Handley Page HP.42 was used on Paris routes, but largely to satisfy the demand for the 'Silver Wing' service, which offered high levels of comfort and luxury, rather than due to its speed. Paris was also the first en-route point on the Empire routes. It was left to others to try and develop new short-haul route opportunities both on UK domestic and non-Imperial European routes.

The UK domestic aviation scene was not short of companies trying to become established, but with thin routes and unsuitable aircraft, few lasted more than a year or two. Several were motor hire or coach companies trying to break into commercial aviation, but their principal competitors were the railway companies, all of whom enjoyed a well-established route network across the UK and guarded it jealously. They were formidable and financially strong competitors and without some form of subsidy it was very difficult for new airline entrants to survive. Railway Air Services was one of the better operators, supported by some of the railway companies that took shareholdings and injected capital, hence the name. Even Imperial Airways had railway company minority shareholders for a time.

Northern Europe was another matter, and provided opportunities with only limited competition from foreign airlines. A new private company,

British Airways Ltd, backed by investment capital, set out to become a 'second force' British international airline and establish its own sphere of influence in Northern Europe. Services to Copenhagen and Stockholm were begun in 1936, followed by a subsidised night mail service to Germany in 1937. As the busiest air route in the world at the time, Paris was also seen as an opportunity, but as this was Imperial Airways' territory the services were operated in conjunction with them.

A British Airways Ltd Lockheed L-14 Super Electra at Berlin (Tempelhof), late 1930s.

Above and left: A British Airways Ltd Lockheed L-10 Electra (main image) and L-14 Super Electra, both at Heston. These all-metal construction, twin-engine monoplanes set new standards of speed, reliability and reduced engineering maintenance.

STEP INTO EUROPE WITH
BRITISH AIRWAYS

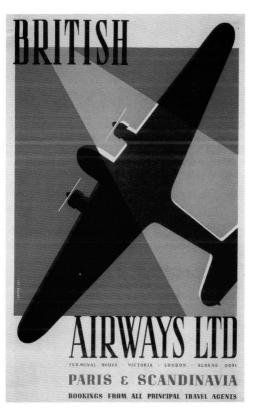

Above left: British Airways Ltd was the businessman's airline of the 1930s. Speed was certainly an important factor for the longer distances to northern Germany and Scandinavia, and flying allowed a round-trip business journey to be easily accomplished in a day.

Above middle and right: British Airways Ltd often advertised in a more contemporary modern style, using new colour photographic techniques as well as artists. (Theyre Lee-Elliott)

Restructuring

British Airways Ltd did not have things all its own way. Another private British company, British Continental Airways (BCA), began to compete directly on several routes. Both companies were well financed, but at a time when competition between airlines was likely to bankrupt one or both, it was not in the British government's interests to see them fail, not least as it was subsidising the UK–Scandinavia and Germany mail services. British Airways became the preferred government option and BCA was taken over.

With no restriction on buying foreign aircraft, British Airways began to develop its aircraft fleet, purchasing the most technologically up-to-date aircraft, firstly the Dutch Fokker F.XII and then the German Junkers Ju 52. Both were all-metal, three-engine monoplanes, but the most significant new aircraft were the Lockheed L-10A Electra and L-14 Super Electra. These fast, twin-engine, American-built monoplanes set new standards in reliability and maintenance efficiency. Compared to Imperial's ageing fleet of ungainly biplanes (apart from the 'Short 'C' Class flying boats), British Airways looked like a modern airline. Operating principally out of Heston Airport, close to today's Heathrow, British Airways began to be admired as much for its product and services as for its modern management style and entrepreneurial attitude.

By 1939, with the war clouds gathering over Europe, the British government decided that it would be in the national interest to purchase British Airways and merge it with Imperial Airways. From 1 April 1940, the new name in aviation would be British Overseas Airways Corporation (BOAC). Imperial and British Airways would continue operating until then but in a co-operative manner. The expectation was that by linking Imperial's undoubted experience and overall resources with British Airways' flair and leadership, the new BOAC would emerge as a stronger airline, able to assert itself in the future commercial aviation world. The beginning of the Second World War in September 1939 stopped that expectation in its tracks. It would be six long years before BOAC could begin to show itself on the world stage. In between, it had a major role to play in continuing to link Britain with its Empire and its allies in a struggle for survival.

Imperial Airways' Short L.17 entered service in May 1934 and its design was old from the start. Many foreign manufacturers were developing faster and more modern monoplane aircraft, such as the German Junkers Ju 52 and Dutch Fokker F.XII used by, among others, British Airways Ltd and Air France, as seen in this image.

The L.17 could, however, hold its own on short routes such as London–Paris where its large, comfortable cabin provided a very high standard of customer care through the 'Silver Wing' service. Losing a few minutes on short flights was an acceptable penalty for Imperial's customers and the services were often full. (London News Agency)

1920s traditionalism versus 1930s modernism: another example of Imperial's ageing fleet in contrast to the modern Luft Hansa monoplane taking off from Croydon. (Kenneth A. McDonough)

Above: In contrast to the stately biplanes of much of its fleet, Imperial Airways leapt ahead of the competition in 1939 on delivery of the elegant and fast de Havilland Frobisher. While it was one of the fastest aircraft of its time, its main drawback was its wooden construction. Though strong and flexible, wood needs care and the aircraft needed to be kept in a hangar in bad weather or risk damage to its structure.

The aircraft also shows on its nose the Imperial Airways' logo, the 'Speedbird', the first time since its design by Theyre Lee-Elliott in 1932 that it had been shown on an aircraft. (Robert E. Coates Photography)

Left: British Airways Ltd was chosen by the British government to fly the then Prime Minister, Neville Chamberlain, to Munich for a series of meetings with Adolf Hitler in 1938. Prime Minister Chamberlain arrived back at Heston in September that year to great acclaim, promising 'peace in our time', but within a year Great Britain was at war with Germany. (London News Agency)

Merchant Airmen

Although civil air services continued where at all possible following the commencement of hostilities, Imperial Airways and British Airways and the few private UK domestic airlines immediately came under the control of the British Air Ministry. The so-called 'phoney war' of late 1939/early 1940 enabled services to Paris and the nearer European points to continue, as well as services to Africa, the Middle East and Far East, but the threat of wider hostilities forced Imperial and British Airways to move their headquarters from Croydon and Heston respectively to Whitchurch near Bristol, flying boat operations moving to Poole Harbour in Dorset. By early 1940, with the closure of European airspace, routes to the Middle East and beyond were also cut.

The Second World War was a total war in all senses of the imagination. With Britain completely isolated, maintaining links with its Empire and allies became ever more important, and the new BOAC stepped into the breach. BOAC had several things critical to achieving its new role: experienced crews, engineers and support staff and a wealth of knowledge and resourcefulness in how to get things done with minimal resources in out-of-the-way places. These attributes and more would be needed as the orders for support and supplies flooded in and kept up a relentless momentum until 1945. Although many air services began resumption in early 1945, it would not be until 1 January 1946 that restrictions on civil flying in British airspace were lifted.

Merchant Airmen is the British Air Ministry's account of British civil aviation between 1939 and 1944. It is a graphic account of the many crucial roles performed by BOAC and others in support of the Allied war effort. A few pages of print and images in this book cannot do justice to the skill and endeavour of BOAC's people in those long years of adversity, but from the struggle and debris of war there emerged activities that would shape the future of civil aviation. They would be important markers for the resumption of civil air services and provide a foundation upon which BOAC could build a successful company.

Of particular importance was the development of skill sets and experience in piloting and engineering that would be invaluable in re-establishing commercial air services when the war ended. The UK–US route had started to be flown commercially in August 1939, but only for airmail. The route had also never been flown in winter, but this had to be accomplished in order to ferry pilots back to Canada and the USA following their eastbound delivery flights of military aircraft needed for the war effort. In November 1940 BOAC made the first proving flights, and in May 1941 the more difficult westbound route was flown by the RAF and then taken over by BOAC in September. The North Atlantic Return Ferry Service, as it became known, continued uninterrupted six days a week, year round for the rest of the war. When the service ended in September 1946 over 2,000 crossings had been made, a remarkable record of endurance, reliability and airmanship, especially during the bitter North American winters.

The role of women again took centre stage as the men went off to fight. With aircraft taking a pivotal role and with combat pilots in short supply, BOAC put forward the idea of an Air Transport Auxiliary (ATA) to ferry aircraft of all types from factories and storage depots to the forward airfields. Recruiting both male pilots unfit for combat duties and female pilots, BOAC administered a hugely successful operation, with over 300,000 delivery sectors flown and with very few aircraft lost. Although the female pilots of the ATA were demobbed without any fanfare at the end of the war, they had shown what could be done. Similarly, female wartime engineers did not so easily fit in at the factories and workshops during peacetime when the men returned. It would take several more decades before being a pilot or an aircraft engineer became a realistic career choice for women, but the die had been cast and there would be no turning back.

It was maybe a little easier for BOAC's first female cabin attendants. Recruited during the war, they stayed on as stewardesses when commercial flying restarted in 1946. BOAC had realised that if they were to compete with the powerful American airlines who were expected to start services to Europe once the war ended, they would need to improve their product offering. The pre-war standards offered by their predecessors would not do and male and female cabin crew would both be an important part of the new travel experience. The American airlines had moved beyond the standards of the 1930s and were highly experienced in customer expectations from operating long-haul US domestic services throughout the war years. Comfort in the air would be centre stage once again, but to standards that reflected modern contemporary design rather than the chintz and lace and cut glass of a past age.

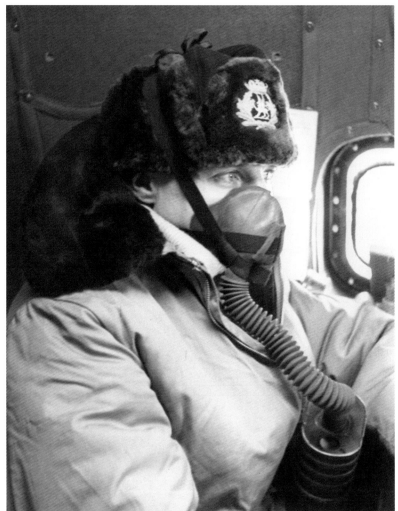

Above and right: A Consolidated Liberator aircraft of BOAC's North Atlantic Return Ferry Service prepares to leave Dorval Airfield, Montreal, in the early 1940s. Winter flying conditions were extremely challenging, but BOAC's ferry service rarely failed to get through. Equally challenging were the cabin standards, with thick coats and blankets necessary, and sometimes oxygen, in the unheated aircraft.

 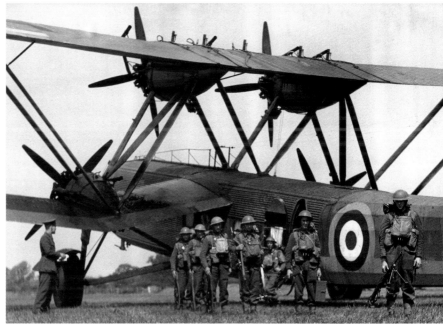

Above left: A previously unseen photograph of Prime Minister Winston Churchill lunching with the First Sea Lord, Admiral of the Fleet Sir Dudley Pound, and Lord Beaverbrook. The photograph was privately taken on board a BOAC Boeing 314 flying boat returning from Bermuda to the UK following Churchill's meeting with US President Roosevelt in January 1942. Unseen are the rest of the Joint Chiefs of Staff who were also on board, an enormous responsibility for BOAC and the aircraft's crew under Captain Kelly Rogers. Lord Beaverbrook had spoken to Captain Kelly Rogers before the flight and said, 'If we lose Churchill we lose the war.' No pressure then, but Captain Kelly Rogers and his crew performed the journey with all the professionalism and skill that epitomised BOAC's contribution to the war effort. (E. O. Draper)

Above right: An ex-Imperial Airways HP.42 disembarks British troops somewhere in England. The aircraft is possibly G-AAXF *Helena*, which was taken over for military service as part of BOAC's support for the war effort. (Brooklands Museum Photographic Archive)

Above: BOAC's Avro York G-AGJC at Cape Town, 24 March 1945, with Captain O. P. Jones and his crew in the foreground. By early 1945, the Mediterranean route was open again and more direct routings to Africa and the Middle/Far East could be operated.

Left: A female Air Transport Auxiliary pilot prepares to depart to deliver a Typhoon fighter-bomber to a forward airfield. Four-engine bombers, fighters and transport aircraft were all in a day's work for the pilots of the ATA; they flew anything and everything, often with no prior experience, and relied purely on their flying skill and a 'can-do' attitude to get them through.

207 Aircraft, Mostly Unsuitable

BOAC's war ended with a collection largely made up of converted wartime military aircraft. This was not quite the situation Imperial Airways faced twenty years earlier, but most were rapidly becoming obsolete, with seven types of flying boats and the rest land planes, with an assortment of at least nineteen different engines. Most were also at the end of their useful lives, having received hard treatment during their wartime service. The flying boats were the remnants of a successful era but one now rapidly coming to an end. With many more airfields now available following their rapid development across the world during the war years, there was little future need for flying boats.

Just as Imperial Airways had to do in 1924, BOAC needed to rapidly rationalise its fleet and evaluate what future types it needed. While it retained a role to link the UK with its Empire, which was soon to shrink rapidly, BOAC was to have a much wider remit; it was intended to facilitate trade with the UK, be a showcase for British aviation and engineering skill and, in due course, cover its costs and maybe pay a dividend to the UK Treasury. Although the Empire routes remained important, the prime route was the North Atlantic. While BOAC had a vast amount of operational experience in crossing the North Atlantic during the war, peacetime operations needed not only new aircraft and equipment but a comprehensive US-based commercial organisation and operational facilities. Organisational change to reflect a new, commercially orientated company took centre stage, but it was a slow process. BOAC knew that if it was to have any chance of success it had to become a carrier of choice across its network. This would take time to develop, as its brand and products were not widely known and of inferior quality to its main US competitors.

A major problem was that BOAC was required to buy British aircraft, but there was nothing suitable that could provide any sort of competitive product. The UK aircraft manufacturers had been totally geared up for wartime production and were not able to produce anything in the short term other than conversions of wartime bombers. The new Avro Tudor civilian aircraft would be available in 1947 and was the UK government's preferred option for BOAC, but it did not meet the airline's specification and would require numerous modifications. The US Lockheed Constellation 049 was the aircraft of choice for BOAC's competitors and BOAC had to match them. Very reluctantly, the UK government agreed and two 049s were authorised to be purchased for delivery in early 1946, with three more to follow. The Constellation would provide the competitive product BOAC needed to build its transatlantic operations. Its other long-haul routes would have to make do with a selection of modified aircraft from its wartime fleet until suitable UK aircraft became available. European routes were another matter and would require a different treatment.

Post-war 'make do and mend': modifying the front gun turret made a useful cargo hold for BOAC's Lancastrians.

Following several major design modifications, the first Avro Tudor 2 was delivered to BOAC and christened by the then Princess Elizabeth at Heathrow on 21 January 1947. Named *Elizabeth of England*, the aircraft still failed to perform adequately and later was transferred to British South American Airways.

Above and right: The Avro York was a passenger plane derivative of the Avro Lancaster bomber and a solid and dependable aircraft, if somewhat sparse in creature comforts. It also made a good freighter aircraft and its high wing allowed a large cabin and cargo space. One of the York's more exotic cargoes was five young Siamese elephants destined for Billy Smart's Circus. The flight attracted considerable media interest, being the first time elephants had ever been carried by air.

BOAC subsequently produced a small brochure, *The Five Flying Elephants*, reproducing a report by the *Daily Express* reporter Bernard Wicksteed. The report tells us that, apparently, elephants make bad sailors and suffer from seasickness, so many now go by air. There was not a lot of room left in the aircraft for extra trunks and, after more than thirty-nine hours in the air with many stops en route, probably not a lot of fresh air either. (Cartoon graphic by Burt)

Above and left: BOAC's Lockheed Constellation G-AHEM *Balmoral* was one of five Constellations that operated the first scheduled flights between London and New York, commencing on 1 July 1946. These early North Atlantic flights were routed either via Shannon or Glasgow then Reykjavik and Gander for refuelling, a total journey time westbound of twenty hours at a one-way fare of £86.85. By 1948 the frequency had increased from four to six weekly, but BOAC just did not have enough aircraft to fly more services.

Opposite left: BSAA was the third nationalised UK airline, set up in 1946 to operate routes to the Caribbean and South America, and operated the very first flight out of the new London Airport (Heathrow) when it opened on 1 January 1946. BSAA suffered from the same uncompetitive aircraft as BOAC but was unable to buy a more modern fleet and operated 'thin' routes with low passenger numbers; after several years of financial losses, BSAA was merged into BOAC in 1949.

Opposite right: As it had little else to use, BOAC continued to operate Hythe flying boats when it reopened the UK–Australia route in conjunction with Qantas after the Second World War. Qantas operated modern Constellations and was not impressed with BOAC offering an inferior product as part of the joint service.

BEA: The Key to Europe

With BOAC's main focus on developing its long-haul routes, there was always the risk it would take Europe less seriously, as some believed Imperial Airways had done. Given the importance of Europe to the UK in the immediate post-war period, it was a risk that could not be taken. European route development was taken from BOAC and given to a new UK state corporation, British European Airways (BEA), to be the second UK nationalised airline. BEA's remit was to develop not only routes to Europe but all UK domestic services, including the essential Highlands and Islands services. Like BOAC, it was given a route monopoly and the few UK private scheduled airlines that still existed, such as Railway Air Services, were bought and merged into BEA.

BOAC had initiated European services in early 1946 to the main Western European capitals using its wartime DC3 aircraft, and these were transferred to BEA and supplemented by the new, UK-built Vickers Viking aircraft, a short-haul, twin-engine aircraft based on the Wellington bomber. While the Viking appeared to be yet another modification of a military aircraft, it was far more than that and very fit for purpose. Large parts of Europe were shattered during the Second World War, not just economically but politically and socially. European air travel for the first few years would be more about providing a fast and convenient means of getting from A to B at a reasonable price and the frills could come later. The Vikings were solid workhorses, able to take the lumps and bumps of rough, damaged runways with minimal maintenance facilities and had the advantage of 'coming home at night' back to their UK base for any major repairs.

The UK aviation industry was much better at producing short-haul aircraft and BEA had nothing like the issues facing BOAC, which desperately needed US-built aircraft to offer a competitive product. BEA could 'buy British' without being seriously compromised, having several suitable aircraft types to choose from and with several prospects on the drawing board for later years. Like BOAC, however, BEA also had to suffer the UK's arcane government procurement process, which assessed, and then told the two corporations, what aircraft they should buy, despite having little real commercial or operational knowledge upon which to base their decisions; it was all about supporting the UK aircraft manufacturers rather than the operating airlines.

BEA operated out of an RAF airfield at Northolt pending a progressive move to Heathrow during the early 1950s. At least it had some prefab buildings to operate from rather than the early tents at Heathrow, although its nearby head office was an old school building.

BEA's proving flight to Montpellier on 13 April 1949 was flown by Captain W. Baillie in a Vickers Viking. The aircraft was met by Commandant Audibert, the commandant of the Montpellier-Frejorgues airport, seen here with Captain Baillie and his crew. Grass, earth or concrete landing fields were all the same to the robust Viking. (Midi-Libre)

Building the Infrastructure

Croydon had been London's main airport during the 1920s and 1930s and a fighter airfield during the war. It was not, however, capable of being expanded to the extent needed for the development of civil aviation envisaged once the war ended. The pan-flat farmlands around the village of Heath Row to the west of London provided an ideal location, with space to expand in future years as traffic demands grew. The runways began to be laid in 1944 and by 1 January 1946 the first experimental flight by BSAA left the new London Airport (Heathrow) for Buenos Aires. On 28 May 1946 BOAC operated the first commercial flight, this time to Australia. All passengers checked in at what became known as 'tent city', on the A4 Bath Road north of the airport; while the tents were quite quickly replaced by prefabricated buildings, it would be nearly ten years before the first passenger terminal building (Europa) opened in 1955 in what became called London Airport Central Area. BEA moved from Northolt to Heathrow progressively during the early 1950s, but BOAC continued to operate out of the north-side prefabs for a while longer, until a separate terminal was completed for long-haul operations.

Both BOAC and BEA had, in the late 1940s, begun to establish new engineering facilities to the east of Heathrow at Hatton Cross, but the facilities were not shared and were completely separate. The rivalry between the two companies was apparent even in these early years. Many in BOAC considered BEA a bit of a 'poor relation', operating mostly rather unglamorous routes to war-torn Europe with a ragbag collection of aircraft. This was an unsustainable point of view once BEA became well established and developed into what many considered 'the Number 1 in Europe', but the prejudice remained, unfairly, for many years.

The late 1940s was an age of austerity in the UK, which the grey, windswept acres of Heathrow rather emphasised. The summer of 1946 was very wet; the tents leaked, mud was underfoot and mosquitoes bred in the deep puddles between the duckboards. The customer experience was challenging to say the least, but passengers accustomed to the rigours of the war years could be more stoic and accepting of the lack of creature comforts that we would take for granted today. BEA fared a little better at Northolt; they at least had concrete underfoot and a solid roof, but with their main offices located in an old school building at Ruislip close to the airport perimeter, there were few frills on offer. BEA's one class of travel and on-board service was more basic and reflective of the time, a period of severe shortages of many products and services and a continuation of UK food rationing.

Overall, Heathrow was being shaped to become the premier airport for London and the main operating base for BOAC and BEA as the two nationalised UK airlines. This advantage would have tremendous influence and benefit in the coming years.

Opposite top left: Railway Air Services survived the war years but not BEA's takeover in 1946. Operating between Glasgow and London via Belfast and several Midland cities, RAS used a fleet of de Havilland biplanes, a 1930s design that was economic for the 'thin' routes it flew and robust; several of the 'Rapide' and 'Dragon' versions are still flying today.

Opposite below left: BEA became the preferred airline for the 1948 London Olympic Games just as British Airways did sixty-four years later. In this image, BEA Captain C. B. Wright receives the Olympic torch from the film star Linden Travers in conjunction with the flying of the official Olympic film from London to Europe for distribution to European cinemas.

Opposite right: BEA produced a number of passenger information brochures in the late 1940s with attractive contemporary graphics, this one promoting its services as 'Key to the Air', a play on its motto, *'Clavis Europa'*, or 'Key to Europe'.

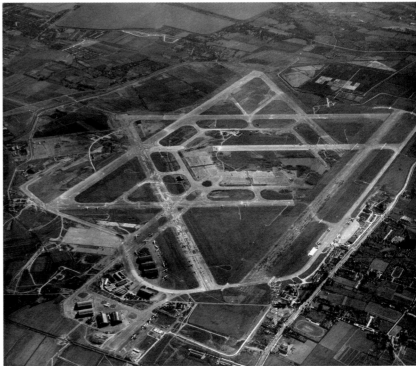

Above left: 'Tent city', London Airport (Heathrow) north side, 1946. Not a military camp but what would become the UK's premier airport. It would be unthinkable today to build an airport without passenger terminal facilities, but these were austere times following the end of the Second World War and the priority was to re-establish air links with the world and develop trade. The fancy bits could come later.

Above right: London Airport (Heathrow), late 1940s. The long-haul arrival and departure buildings are to the right of the picture, alongside the A4 Bath Road. BOAC's engineering facilities also begin to take shape in the bottom-left corner. The airport's Central Area remained a building site with no usable passenger facilities until 1955, when the new Europa Terminal opened.

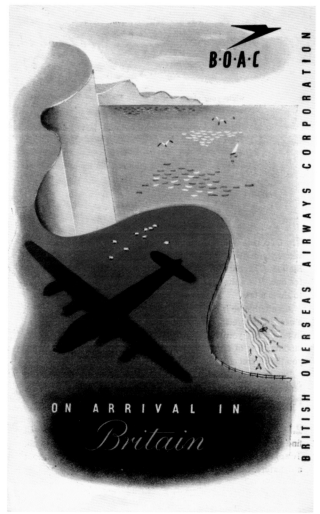

Above: Pre-departure refreshments at London (Heathrow) north side, late 1940s. Smart waiters and personal service were prerequisites for BOAC's early clientèle, albeit the facilities were more pavement café than the Ritz.

Right: A 1947 BOAC passenger brochure on what to expect in post-war Britain and what restrictions passengers would have to cope with. Visitors to the UK could otherwise have little idea whether there would be transport or hotels, let alone basics such as food and clothing. Rationing was still in force and would be until the early 1950s, and everyone needed to register for an identity card and food coupons – even foreign visitors.

Developing the Brand

In 1946, BOAC established a high-level design committee to set the standards for a new-look, post-war airline that would reflect the changing face of a modern world but retain the high standards and customer expectations of its predecessors. The airline recognised that it needed to establish a common identity across its services and products, from signage to chinaware and uniforms to aeroplane liveries. Developing the brand would be an evolving process but would retain for many years one early element: the Speedbird logo, designed in 1932 for Imperial Airways.

BEA's approach was more utilitarian, but by the end of the 1940s it began to differentiate its services both in appearance and content. A new livery was brought in to replace the unpainted fuselages of its early fleet and interiors began to be improved as part of an overall service uplift. The various aircraft fleets were renamed and each aircraft carried the name of 'famous British male persons', although none living so as 'to avoid envy, hatred, malice and all uncharitableness'! The new Airspeed Ambassador aircraft expected in 1951 were to become the 'Elizabethan' fleet. Clearly looking ahead to the prospects of the then HRH Princess Elizabeth eventually becoming queen, the rationale was that it represented what was 'the most famous period in British history ... and may be again one day' – an insightful perception.

BEA also pioneered attracting new business by the introduction of night fares at considerable discounts. For both BOAC and BEA, early services were just one class until the early 1950s and night fares and special fares for service personnel were attempts to widen the travel base and provide a more comprehensive and affordable service for prospective passengers.

BOAC and BEA came to represent the 'New Age' that was developing across society during the late 1940s and early 1950s, a period of rapidly accelerating economic, social and political change. Air travel was at the forefront of this period. It evoked modernity and style, a moving forward with the prospect of new opportunities as the horrors of the war years began gradually to recede and European and world economies began to rebuild.

The principles that applied in these early years, based on the concept of good design, innovation and the creation of lasting values, are still applied today by British Airways in its current design guidelines.

A BSAA 'Star Girl', as its stewardesses were known, serves pre-dinner drinks and canapés on an Avro Tudor. BSAA tried hard to make its operation a success but the combination of few passengers, poor aircraft economics and sheer bad luck made it an impossible task. It was merged into BOAC in 1949.

Although never implemented, the interior design for BOAC's abortive Avro Tudor was very forward-looking, with the use of brighter colours and a style that would do credit to the 1970s. The modern design reflected the work of BOAC's new design committee, industrial designer Richard Lonsdale-Hands and the influence of designer F. H. K. Henrion, who was engaged as the committee's consultant. (R. Lonsdale-Hands/J. Tandy)

No. 7. October 1946

B·O·A·C
NEWS LETTER [SPEEDBIRD]

HOUSE JOURNAL OF BRITISH OVERSEAS AIRWAYS CORPORATION

MISS B.O.A.C. STEPS OUT [see page 3]

Far left: BOAC and BEA did collaborate on some advertising, possibly because the UK government continued to interfere, complaining that the two corporations were wasting money by not combining their advertising where appropriate. (F. H. K. Henrion)

Left: BOAC's early uniforms reflected their military origins and were originally supplied by Austen Reid. BOAC management were keen that their first female stewardesses were not seen just as glamorous assistants to the cabin stewards but hard-working and equal members of an aircraft's crew, hence a very male-orientated uniform design and the application of strict wearer standards. By the early 1950s, the tie and belt were dispensed with and the style had relaxed and softened under the influence of the British designer Maurice Helman.

Above: The folder of a set of useful in-flight amenity leaflets handed out to BOAC passengers in the late 1940s. The folder's attractive artwork was another example of encouraging their being taken away by passengers as a memento of their flight, and a reminder to fly on BOAC again. (Alan V.)

Left: A BOAC Monarch service menu from the early 1950s. Early menus were artworks in themselves as an encouragement to passengers to take them home as a reminder of their journey. (H. Schwarz)

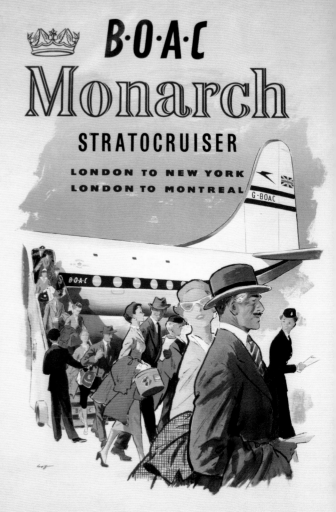

B·O·A·C
Monarch
STRATOCRUISER
LONDON TO NEW YORK
LONDON TO MONTREAL

G-BOAC

B·O·A·C

BRITISH OVERSEAS AIRWAYS CORPORATION

Above and opposite right: By the late 1940s, BOAC had again forced the UK government to allow it to buy the latest US aircraft, the Boeing Stratocruiser. The Stratocruiser was a step up in style and comfort, harking back to the 1930s with luxury cabins, a lounge and even folding, full-length beds; it was the perfect aircraft for BOAC's first-class Monarch service on the important North Atlantic route. (Goz)

Right: BEA's early 1960s forces fares advertising, in a style that was very much of its time, to encourage the large British forces contingent based in West Germany to fly home rather than drive.

Opposite left: A BEA publicity shoot in 1952, introducing the new Airspeed Ambassador aircraft in a new BEA livery. BEA named the aircraft type the Elizabethan, but quite what Henry VIII would have thought of it we will never know; he would probably have appreciated the fine dining on the 'Silver Wing' service that BEA reintroduced that year on the London–Paris route using the Elizabethan. The stewardess, Mary Hughes, is wearing BEA's smart, pale-grey uniform of the time, reflecting the more contemporary modern 'New Look' styling that was beginning to dominate women's fashion in the early 1950s.

The End of Empire

The end of the 1940s marked the departure of most of BOAC's older wartime aircraft. By contrast, BEA's original Viking and DC3 (Pionair) fleets soldiered on until 1954 and 1962 respectively, the latter an amazing record for an early aircraft, reflecting its robust characteristics and reasonable performance.

It was truly the end of Empire for the flying boats. The days of Imperial Airways Short 'C' Class Empire flying boats had waxed and waned, with the last surviving aircraft being withdrawn from service by BOAC in 1947; the type had given sterling service for over ten years but was now technologically obsolescent, although the UK government persisted in pressing the case for a giant flying boat able to cross the Atlantic non-stop, the Saunders Roe SR45. BOAC was able to resist being forced to buy the SR45 and retired its last boat, the Short Solent, in 1950.

Above: Casting off, a Short Solent flying boat leaves Southampton dock.

Right: BOAC and South African Airways jointly advertised the UK–South Africa route in the late 1940s, sharing the revenue under a commercial 'pooling' agreement, a common arrangement in the early days of route development between two countries that had single international state airlines.

Opposite left: Farewell after sixteen long years. A BEA DC3 (far right) shares the tarmac at Glasgow's Renfrew Airport in May 1962 on its commemorative flight.

Opposite right: The Short Solent was used on Far East and Southern African routes, where the infrastructure for flying boat operations was well established and land plane operations had yet to develop fully. This late 1940s BOAC poster by Roland Hilder stirs the imagination and captures the allure and promise of the East. (Roland Hilder)

It may have been the end of Empire but it was the blossoming of the new British Commonwealth. Having recently been crowned, HM The Queen accompanied by Prince Philip embarked on a World Commonwealth tour on 23 November 1953. Flying on the first sector to Bermuda in a BOAC Stratocruiser, this charming picture shows Her Majesty descending the steps of the aircraft, shortly to greet the Governor of Bermuda, Sir Alexander Hood.

The Next Generation

The 1950s heralded the next generation in air transport in several distinctive ways. Rapid advances in technology were to provide faster, larger aircraft designed specifically for civilian use. UK and European society was also rapidly changing, reflecting the trends across the Atlantic for a less deferential, free-speaking and better-educated population with more disposable income and the freedom and curiosity to wish to travel abroad. Both BOAC and BEA were well placed to take advantage of the opportunities this presented given their monopoly positions and the growing demand for air travel, both for business and leisure. The economic benefits of larger aircraft operating in the future with improved utilisation and increased passenger and cargo load factors was well understood by both companies. 'Passenger potential' was seen as the key, with increased aircraft range allowing longer, faster sectors and the omission of intermediate stops, thus encouraging more people to travel at cheaper prices.

BEA began to exploit the growing pressure for cheaper fares, particularly to the Mediterranean sun spots, and BOAC to the wealthier, long-haul US and Caribbean markets. In 1952, under pressure from the US airlines, BOAC introduced a US$270 one-way tourist fare on an experimental basis between New York and London. The result was an instant success; capacity was expanded to meet demand and the tourist fare concept was also introduced to other routes. By the 1953 summer season, over 90 per cent of BEA's international capacity was sold as tourist class, with considerable fare reductions.

The next generation also heralded the desire for greater competition in UK air services. In 1953, the UK Conservative government took the opportunity to remove BEA's scheduled service monopoly on UK domestic routes. Within a year over twenty new UK airlines were flying those routes. The future shape of a rapidly changing aviation world was beginning to develop. BOAC and BEA would need to work harder and innovate to keep up, let alone keep ahead of their new competitors.

Above: BEA took every advantage to promote the new lower fares and encourage traffic. Some of its routes had low volumes, especially on UK domestic routes such as Scotland, and it needed to counter the competition from the new and rapidly growing independent UK domestic airlines. (Kenneth Rowntree)

Left: BOAC's first tourist-class services were introduced in 1952, with a New York–London one-way fare of US$270. The services were an instant success.

The Jet Age

On 2 May 1952, BOAC operated the world's first pure jet scheduled passenger air service from London to Johannesburg, flying a de Havilland Comet 1. Cruising at nearly 500 miles per hour at a height of 40,000 feet, it offered an entirely new flying experience at a speed faster than any propeller-driven aircraft. Although the Comet 1 did not have the range to fly the Atlantic, routes to Africa, India and the Far East, which allowed refuelling en route, were ideal. As the lead customer, BOAC was far in front of its competitors and its future appeared bright.

The Comet 1 appeared at last to vindicate the UK government's insistence that its nationalised airlines should 'buy British'. Up to now, BOAC had forced concessions to allow it to purchase US- and Canadian-built aircraft, without which it would have been hopelessly uncompetitive. Even with the first Constellations, however, BOAC was not allowed to purchase enough aircraft to operate more than six US services a week against the US airlines' eighty services, a very frustrating situation. While BOAC fully recognised the desirability of achieving a successful British aircraft industry and worked closely with the manufacturers to help achieve that, without the freedom to make its own purchasing decisions it was fighting a losing battle both in terms of product and financial return. This situation plagued BOAC for many years.

The promise of the Comet 1 tragically failed to materialise. After an encouraging start, slashing journey times wherever it flew, two aircraft were lost and the aircraft was grounded. Structural failure was found to be the cause and the aircraft needed to be redesigned. This was a serious commercial and operational blow for BOAC, which, at a stroke, lost over 20 per cent of its fleet capacity. It would take several years to re-equip and recover, and BOAC's competitive edge was lost.

Above: Fast but flawed. Three Comets fly in formation as part of an early promotional shoot for BOAC.

Opposite left: En route to Johannesburg, a Comet 1 is welcomed by camels. The ships of the desert meet, for the first time, the new star in the aviation sky.

Opposite right: Welcome back. The loss of the Comet 1 meant BOAC quickly had to bring back aircraft recently retired and find a modern replacement pending the Comet's redesign, not expected for several years. The Stratocruisers stayed on until well into the late 1950s and were subsequently joined by the Douglas DC-7C, on the left of this picture, used as a stopgap until the Britannia, on the right, came into service.

British is Best

While the failure of the Comet 1 had hit BOAC hard, the introduction by BEA in 1953 of the Vickers Viscount was a major success story that lasted for many years. Several of the later variants were even operated by British Airways for a short while in the 1970s. The Viscount was itself another step forward in aviation technology, this time largely due to its engines. Powered by four Rolls-Royce Dart turbo-prop engines, this was a new design of part-jet, part-propeller-driven engine technology where the jet part drives the propeller, giving improved speed and economy. The cabin was large and comfortable, initially in an all-first-class configuration, with large windows giving panoramic views. The aircraft was an immediate hit with BEA's passengers.

The Viscount at the time was the UK's most successful aircraft, with over 450 sold worldwide. It gave BEA the opportunity to expand its route network beyond Europe, much to the annoyance of BOAC, which considered it was going beyond its designated 'sphere of influence', i.e. Europe and UK domestic operations. There had been frequent arguing between the two airlines about where their respective traffic boundaries lay, which came to a head in 1954 when BEA sought to take over the Middle East routes from BOAC so that it could operate to Iraq, Iran, Ethiopia and the Middle East generally. BOAC protested vigorously and even suggested the matter be solved by a merger, but this was rejected by the UK government and a compromise agreement reached that BEA would not operate beyond a line east of Cairo/Nicosia/Ankara. When BOAC had to stop services to Tel Aviv following the loss of the Comet 1, BEA stepped in and the route became a sore point for many years, only effectively solved upon the formation of British Airways in 1974.

The Airspeed Ambassador was BEA's other new aircraft, introduced in 1952. Named the 'Elizabethan', it was never the success the Viscount became, but its spacious cabin and high wing, allowing uninterrupted views, did make it popular with passengers. BEA used the Ambassador to reintroduce Imperial Airway's 'Silver Wing' branded service between London and Paris and several other European destinations. The 'Silver Wing' was very popular on Paris but less so elsewhere. The luxurious on-board meals and additional cabin crew provided a high level of quality and personal customer care, especially as the seat capacity was reduced to forty and the flying time to Paris extended by ten minutes to allow for a more relaxed meal service.

The Vickers Viscount and Airspeed Ambassador (Elizabethan) aircraft became the mainstays of BEA's fleet in the 1950s. This fine painting by Frank Wootton shows the two aircraft types at Heathrow's Europa Terminal. (Frank Wootton)

Above: A promotional brochure for the Airspeed Ambassador (Elizabethan) that was used by BEA to reintroduce the Imperial Airways 'Silver Wing' luxury service.

Above and left: The Viscount had very high passenger appeal, with its quiet cabin and large picture windows offering excellent views; promotions of the time often featured these attractions. (*Left:* Frank Wootton)

Opposite: The Bristol Britannia was late in delivery and overshadowed by the introduction of the Comet 4 and Boeing 707, but nevertheless was well liked by passengers for its comfort and quiet cabin, customer service features that, for some, outweighed the slower speed.

The Way Forward

By the mid-1950s, the demand for international air travel was growing rapidly. Airlines increased capacity and new ways were sought to encourage further growth and to make air travel generally easier. This period established the foundation of modern aviation, with close industry co-operation via the industry body IATA in many procedural and technical areas. Without such facilitation measures, it would have been very complicated and potentially expensive to organise travel via several different airlines around the world. Pricing across most international routes was also carried out collaboratively via IATA, but remained subject to government scrutiny. The process, while considered anti-competitive today, did provide a forum for debate over new ideas about fares and cargo rates in these early years of modern aviation. Innovative pricing schemes such as family discounts and ticket-purchase credit plans were introduced via IATA, particularly to encourage off-peak travel and to chip away at the large volumes of travellers who still went by ship across the long-haul routes; 95 per cent of travel to Australia was still by ship in 1955, 89 per cent to South Africa and over 50 per cent across the Atlantic.

The big break, though, came in 1958 with the introduction of economy-class fares on the North Atlantic at a 20 per cent discount off tourist fares. The demand was instant and by the year's end BOAC experienced a 30 per cent increase in its total transatlantic business. Such an increase necessitated yet more capacity, which BOAC would have struggled to meet only a year or two earlier as it sought to make up for the loss of capacity caused by the Comet 1 failure, but a phoenix was to arise from those ashes in the shape of the new Comet 4.

On 4 October 1958, BOAC reintroduced the jet age, operating the redesigned, long-range Comet 4 between London and New York. Jet operations were by now considered the way forward and the days of propeller-driven aircraft would rapidly decline. Unfortunately for BOAC,

it had only recently taken delivery of the Bristol Britannia, a large, turbo-prop-driven aircraft. Although well liked by passengers for its quiet and comfortable cabin (it was nicknamed 'the Whispering Giant'), it was several years late in delivery and would be unable to compete against the new jet aircraft coming into service. Like many of its predecessor aircraft that did not meet expectations, the Britannia would end its days much sooner than expected, flying charter operations with the gradually increasing number of UK independent airlines.

Rapidly following the introduction of the Comet 4 on the North Atlantic was the Boeing 707. With a larger overall capacity than the Comet 4 and slightly faster, the 707 would remain the dominant commercial aircraft for the next decade. Although the Comet 4 became a success, primarily on BOAC's African and Eastern routes, and was competitive, the 707 had taken the edge off the Comet's return.

B·O·A·C
COMET 4 → JETLINER

SUPREME JET COMFORT

BRITISH OVERSEAS AIRWAYS CORPORATION

Above and left: The introduction by BOAC of the Comet 4 inaugurated jet travel on the North Atlantic route. The new aircraft also swiftly flew back to Japan, a jet route pioneered by the Comet 1, where it received new acclaim and became a common sight into the 1960s. (*Above:* Frank Wootton)

Opposite left: The Comet 4 cabin interior décor was by the designer Gaby Schreiber, appointed in 1957 as the aircraft interior design consultant to BOAC's design committee. Everything inside the aircraft, from the soft furnishings to visible interior surfaces, received a subtle patterning of colour, shade and tone to create a restful atmosphere throughout the passenger cabins and restrooms.

FLY B·O·A·C Britannia
JET-PROP AIRLINER

ACROSS THE ATLANTIC

SERVING

LONDON NEW YORK
MONTREAL DETROIT CHICAGO
SAN FRANCISCO

*The fastest, smoothest, most spacious
jet-prop airliner in the world*

BRITISH OVERSEAS AIRWAYS CORPORATION

Travel made easy

See your BOAC Appointed Travel Agent.

He's the man with all the information on BOAC schedules. He can book you by BOAC 707.

Welcome aboard
the ✈ **BOAC**
Rolls-Royce 707

Power by
Rolls-Royce

Superb engines for a superb airliner! The BOAC 707's four Rolls-Royce Conway jets – famous engines with a long tradition of reliability – sweep you along smoothly, effortlessly, high above the world and the weather.

You may book through

No booking fee

Printed in Great Britain   69/A3/76m/Chr.

Above and right: Even though air travel was becoming affordable for the man in the street by the late 1950s, many people had never flown at all. It was something other people did and was best left to them and to birds. To tap into this market an airline's experience and professionalism was often used as a persuasive advertising tool, coupled with the new economy fares and air/sea holiday promotions.

Opposite: The Boeing 707 became the mainstay of BOAC's long-haul fleet in the early 1960s. Larger than the Comet 4, it provided more capacity on the important North Atlantic routes.

The Swinging Sixties

The 1960s was a decade of change for aviation and for society generally. It was the true start of the jet age, which had been prematurely hailed but not delivered by the ill-fated Comet 1.

By 1960, BOAC's first 707s were delivered and replaced the Comet 4s on transatlantic services. The 707s were larger aircraft configured to operate with up to thirty-four first-class seats and ninety-seven economy seats, much-needed extra capacity to meet demand. They would be followed in 1964 by the UK aviation industry's answer to the 707, the Vickers VC10. The VC10 was yet another aircraft pressed upon BOAC by the UK government when it really wanted a common fleet centred on the 707. However, without any large VC10 orders from other airlines, this would have meant Vickers laying off its engineers, which was an unacceptable risk to the government at a time of high unemployment in the UK.

The VC10 did have its positive attributes, however, but at a price as its operating economics were higher than the 707. Offsetting this cost disadvantage was the VC10's superior technology, with a new 'clean wing' design and, for the first time, all four engines placed at the rear of the aircraft. BOAC felt that the increased cruising speed, improved lift and lower landing speed gave the VC10 a six-year advantage over its competitors. This advertising 'puff' was based on some reality, as the aircraft was much liked by passengers for its quiet and comfortable flights, and 'Try a little VC10derness' became a well-known BOAC advertising slogan.

BEA at last could also go jet with the first deliveries in 1960 of the short-haul Comet 4B, a much-needed competitor to the French Caravelle jet used by many of its rival airlines. While the speed of jets over propeller-driven aircraft was less critical on short-haul routes, jet travel was the way to go. The Comet 4B would provide breathing space for BEA until the Hawker Siddeley Trident 1 became available in 1964. Over the next ten years the Trident would be developed through three variants, all used by BEA with some success, and contributed towards BEA's claim to be 'the Number 1 in Europe'.

Travellers were responding to the airlines' increasingly lower-fare offers and more people were now travelling by air than were travelling by ship, to the point that the shipping companies began to look for ways to co-operate rather than compete with air travel; the rise of the UK independent British United Airlines (BUA), an amalgam of small airlines and shipping interests, was one example and a growing threat to both BOAC and BEA. Encouraged by the UK Conservative government to compete on short-haul and, increasingly, long-haul routes, the UK independents would be further encouraged by a new UK Air Transport Licensing Board (ATLB) that introduced a system of competitive route licensing which no longer automatically favoured the nationalised airlines.

Opposite left: 'Jet BOAC to Swinging London' says it all. London's Carnaby Street was the place to be in the mid-1960s and BOAC was ready to take you there.

Opposite right: In the late 1960s, BEA commissioned the British fashion designer Sir Hardy Amies to design a new uniform to complement their new aircraft livery of red wings with a white-and-blue fuselage and quarter Union Flag tail fin design. Introduced in 1968, the 'red riding hood' coat and dark-blue suited uniform stood out on the tarmacs of Europe and very much complemented BEA's slogan to be 'Number 1 in Europe'.

Our birds fly
the shortest distance
between 89 European points

Eighty-nine European points equals eighty-nine airports in Europe. That's sixteen more than anyone else flies to. And in each one of these places there are people who want to go to another place. In the fastest, most comfortable, most enjoyable way possible. Which is what our birds are all about. In a BEA plane a banker from Beirut might find himself having a drink with a drummer from Dusseldorf. A geologist from Australia might chat up a big movie-star from Sweden. An Englishman, an Irishman and a Scotsman could all be going to

Copenhagen. Or a French gentleman going home to Paris might find himself next to an extremely attractive French lady also going home to Paris.

All those people, going to all those places, everyday. Our birds join the dots on the map for them. And for millions of others too—more than any other airline in Europe in fact. That's because we know Europe. So when your customers book through Europe, book them with us — British European Airways. They'll enjoy it more—and thank you for it.

BEA

Number 1 in Europe

General Sales Agents in Australia — Qantas

BEA1544

TRIUMPHANTLY **swift silent serene**

THE **B·O·A·C VC10**

Above and left: 'Swift, Silent, Serene.' BOAC's advertising capitalised on the VC10's quiet cabin, a result of placing the engines at the rear of the fuselage. (*Left:* Frank Wootton)

Opposite left: Very much a product of the 'swinging '60s', BOAC's paper dress uniform from 1967 reflected the carefree, informal attitude of the age. Designed in-house and used on routes from New York to the Caribbean, it was not liked by female cabin crew, who felt it was a little too revealing, and it was quickly withdrawn.

Opposite right: BEA had experimented with helicopter operations since the late 1940s using various types, but none were profitable. A niche was eventually found using the large Sikorsky S61 helicopters for the developing North Sea oil rig business and on the Penzance–Scilly Isles route. They were also chartered for heavy lifting work.

This season, we're going way out on our way out to the islands.

Our VC 10's and Rolls-Royce 707 fan jets have been flying to Bermuda, Nassau and Jamaica for years. Now, they're going way out to Antigua and Barbados, too.

That's why we're dressing our stewardesses in wild paper dresses. And covering our headrests with bright orange sunshine. And serving on colorful placemats. And passing out first-class bamboo cups in first-class.

And while this entire island attire will add a lot of fun to your trip, it won't add one penny to your air fare. So if you're planning an island vacation, ask your Travel Agent to include our way out way out.

BOAC
TAKES GOOD CARE OF YOU

BEA BEA Helicopters Limited

Gatwick Airport, Surrey. *Tel:* AVEnue 8711. Penzance Heliport, Cornwall. *Tel: Penzance 3871*

BEA Tridents give your customers more time to enjoy Europe

With every new Trident, BEA is getting bigger. And Europe smaller. Because the Trident is the most advanced aircraft in Europe. It was specially designed and built for BEA. Which means that it's ideal for our routes (to all 89 destinations in Europe). And therefore our passengers. We think of the Trident in terms of its excellent design — inside and out.

Its three powerful Rolls Royce jet engines are all positioned at the rear for quiet cruising at 610 mph. Flight systems and flight deck equipment are triplicated. And the most advanced all-weather landing system in the world means new standards of punctuality and dependability. But we don't want to dazzle you with statistics. Just consider the Trident as a superbly comfortable ride. In almost absolute quiet. And fast. Europe is now no more than five hours from end to end.

So when you book your customers through Europe, book them BEA. We're Europe's Number 1 airline. We fly more people (of all nationalities) to more places with better service than any other airline in Europe. So do yourself a favour — book your customers through Europe on BEA — British European Airways, the people who know Europe. They'll enjoy it more — and thank you for it.

BEA

Number 1 in Europe

General Sales Agents in Australia — Qantas

Opposite: The Hawker Siddeley Trident became the mainstay of the BEA fleet in the later 1960s and early 1970s and performed the world's first fully automated landing on a commercial service in summer 1965, a major technological advance for operations in poor visibility. The later variant, the Trident Three, was not BEA's first choice, however; they preferred the new Boeing 727, which had better operating costs and delivery options. The UK government vetoed the 727 to protect Hawker Siddeley, effectively increasing BEA's costs by several million pounds.

This page: By the late 1960s, new, shorter routes to West Coast USA and the Far East became available, flying over the North Pole or Siberia. These routes could reduce flying times by several hours and laid the foundation for many of today's shorter air journeys.

More than Just an Airline

Apart from BUA, other new UK independent airlines such as Cunard Eagle and Caledonian Airways began to be granted licences to compete for holiday traffic, offering inclusive tour charters. Although charters had restrictive travel conditions to provide some protection to scheduled airlines, they were often ignored. BOAC countered with a commercial deal with the shipping company Cunard on the North Atlantic routes, but the independents continued to undermine the scheduled market, often supported by the sympathetic UK, US and Dutch governments.

In 1969, BEA set up its own inclusive air tour subsidiary, BEA Airtours, in direct competition with the independents, but they were all fighting for a limited share of the same market at prices that could not realistically be sustained. The UK government took matters into its own hands in 1970 and established a new regulatory body, the Civil Aviation Authority, to oversee competition between the UK airlines. The UK also argued the case for the establishment of a 'second force' airline of a sufficient size to become a real competitor to BOAC and BEA. Caledonian Airways was seen as more than just an airline and a realistic 'second force' option. If Caledonian was really going to mean it and deliver, it needed to be bigger and the government encouraged it to take over BUA to form a new airline: British Caledonian Airways.

BEA Airtours operated a fleet of nine Comet 4Bs between the UK and various Mediterranean sunspots. In 1974 it became a wholly owned subsidiary of British Airways and was renamed British Airtours. It was again renamed in 1988 as Caledonian Airways following the acquisition of BCAL.

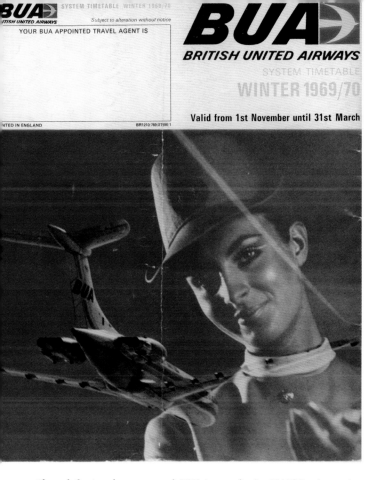

Above left: An almost surreal BUA image for its 1969/70 winter timetable that suggests it was a major player among the UK independent airlines, which, indeed, it was. Operating a profitable holiday charter programme and scheduled services to Europe, Africa and South America, it provided a useful platform for the expansion of Caledonian Airways, who bought BUA in 1970.

Above right: British Caledonian Airways advertised itself as 'more than just an airline', alluding to its place in offering a real choice to customers over the established UK airlines. As the UK CAA's favoured 'second force' airline, it certainly did offer a choice and a very good standard of service, but it was insufficiently different to build market share and allow it to grow without regulatory support.

The Right Aircraft for the Future

The 1970s marked another significant decade of change for the aviation industry. It was becoming increasingly clear that BOAC and BEA could no longer continue as separate companies and be fairly treated by the regulators in this competitive new era. The huge amounts of expertise and overall value to the UK economy and Great Britain established by the two companies over decades would count for nothing in the competitive age that was rapidly dawning. The foundations were being laid for the integration of BOAC and BEA and the formation of British Airways as the new name in aviation.

What British Airways would truly benefit from would be the expertise of its predecessors as well as their route networks and overall assets, particularly their people. The UK government's long-term aim was to establish a world-beating airline and release it from the restrictions of nationalisation. That aim would take several years to achieve, but the prospects appeared bright. Although saddled with a large and diverse fleet, British Airways had the benefit of the new Boeing 747, which came into service with BOAC in 1971. BOAC had considered the 747 the right aircraft for the future and so it proved. Although it was a doubling of capacity over the 707s and VC10s, the reduction in unit costs proved a significant benefit in competition with the new charter companies that had begun to operate on the Atlantic routes.

The introduction of the 747 was probably the most significant change in BOAC's operations since moving from flying boats to land planes. The aircraft was large by any measure, needing not only a major rearrangement of the stands and check-in facilities at Heathrow's Terminal 3 to handle the larger aircraft and volumes of passengers, but also the technical and engineering facilities to look after it. These matters would again take centre stage for British Airways in 2013, when the next generation of very large aircraft, the Airbus A380, was delivered.

MONARCH LOUNGE

CABIN A (FIRST CLASS)

CABIN B (FIRST CLASS)

CABIN C (ECONOMY)

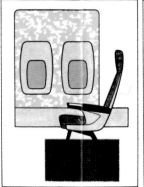

CABIN D (ECONOMY)

CABIN E (ECONOMY)

Getting into
gear
for the '70s

>BOAC

Above: BOAC's first Boeing 747-136, G-AWNA, delivered on 20 April 1970. The adverts of the time made the point that 'all the 747 needed was BOAC service' – the one thing all other 747s already flying did not have. With fifteen cabin crew, it was personalised service indeed.

Right: 'Getting into gear for the '70s': BOAC introduced a new uniform by the British designer Clive Evans to go with the 747. Apart from the need to bring its very old, 1950s-style uniform up to date, the new creation for the first time provided trousers for stewardesses, long winter boots and mix-and-match accessories, very much a sign of the times. A very modern touch was the ability to wash the tropical summer dress uniform in a hotel sink and let it drip-dry overnight, another sign of the 1970s.

Opposite: The sheer size of the 747 gave BOAC's cabin interior designers new opportunities to be creative and personalise the customer experience. Divided into five cabins – two first class and three economy class, plus a 'Monarch' lounge on the upper deck, 'the club in the sky' – the style and décor of each cabin was intended to provide a more intimate and individual but harmonised atmosphere, 'more sitting room in the sky' as it became known.

3

BACK TO THE FUTURE

During 1976, the foundations of the new British Airways had been reviewed, found wanting and reset. The old divisional organisation had been found to be clearly that, divisional. Although some progress had been made in the development of an integrated long-term fleet strategy, the unification of engineering and a common pilot force agreement, closer unity of purpose and real co-operation between the two former workforces was proving painfully slow. British Airways had to present and organise itself as a single face to the outside world, not via three different operational divisions, and so, effective from 1 April 1977, they were swept away. Single departments were created for commercial, flight operations, engineering and planning, with commercial activities based on a structure of route groups, each responsible for the development of their respective revenues and budgets under policies established from the organisation's centre. Apart from departmental name changes to reflect the whims and changing fancies of corporate jargon, the new structure has stood the test of time.

The year 1976 had not been all bad, despite the perceived continued resistance to change. In particular, 21 January 1976 stands out for all those who were at Heathrow that day to see Concorde take off on her first commercial flight to Bahrain. Twenty-seven years later, we would again stand proudly to see Concorde return from her final flights, almost the longest-serving aircraft in the British Airways fleet. Initially, five Concordes were operated with a sixth joining the fleet later. A seventh was put into storage until 1984, when increased fleet utilisation required it being brought into service.

Concorde evolved into a magnificent flagship for British Airways that lifted the company's profile dramatically; flying on Concorde was considered one of the things in life people always wanted to do. It was a hard fight, however, to gain international recognition to allow supersonic flights over land and government restrictions effectively limited the aircraft's economic operation to routes over water. While services to the all-important USA started in 1976 to Washington, the Port Authority of New York tried to stop Concorde operating to the city, but lost its legal battle. The first flight was operated in November 1977 and London to New York became Concorde's key route and the service of choice for the rich and famous and for time-critical business travellers.

Opposite top: 21 January 1976: a series of frames recording British Airways' Concorde G-BOAA rising almost ethereally from Heathrow runway 10R to inaugurate the world's first supersonic commercial air service, between London and Bahrain.

Opposite bottom: The 'Time Machine', as Concorde affectionately became known, is rather psychedelically captured in this advert from 1976. The ad pointed out that leaving London and flying at twice the speed of sound effectively meant arriving in Washington one hour before the time of departure.

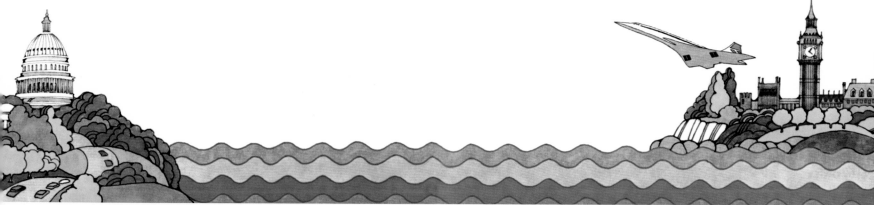

Above: Concorde's flight deck on its inaugural service to Bahrain, signed by Captain Norman Todd, co-pilot Captain Brian Calvert and Senior Engineer Officer John Lidiard.

Right: Concorde's speed advantage was often a central point of its advertising campaigns. 'How times have changed' refers to the much longer flight times of 1952, but in 1976 subsonic flights still took twice as long as Concorde between London and New York. Time-critical customers flying on business were more than willing to pay a premium over normal first-class fares to fly by Concorde. (Foote, Cone & Belding, now Draftfcb London Ltd)

How times have changed.

Twenty-five years ago, a flight to New York took about 11 hours. Now Concorde does the trip daily in just 3½ hours. Doesn't time fly?

British airways

We'll take more care of you.

A Class Apart

'There's something very satisfying about belonging to a club ... there's a sense of camaraderie, the feeling of belonging, the secret delight in enjoying what others can't ... And being a member of British Airways Executive Club is something very special indeed.' The sheer size of the 747 allowed British Airways the interior space to make that advertised claim in May 1977, when the company launched the first Executive Club cabin on its UK–US routes. The 'Club Class' brand was immediately heralded as British Airways' answer to the 'businessmen's blues' and the concept was quickly copied by others under a bewildering variety of brand names; 'Club', however, remains uniquely a British Airways air travel initiative that cannot be taken away.

Possibly not so uniquely successful was the introduction in October 1978 of a completely new style of catering for first-class and Club passengers on the North Atlantic routes, the 'Elizabethan' service. This was not exactly a return to the BEA luxury-service class of the 1950s, which was 'Elizabethan' in name only, but offered a range of traditional Elizabethan food and drink. The stated aim was 'to provide passengers, and in particular those who were visitors to Britain, with a style of cabin service that was different from other airlines while at the same time retaining a specifically English flavour'. It was certainly that. Being treated to authentic Elizabethan dishes and drink from 400 years ago while enjoying the benefits of twentieth-century technology 6 miles over the Atlantic was an eclectic mix at best. While 'real' ale was welcome, 'posset' was an acquired taste. The Club menu for the Washington–London service offered 'Capon Puddynge after mistress Duffeld's way', followed by 'Sherborne apple and orange tarte' and 'Posset Sir Francis'. Quite what was 'mistress Duffeld's way' is unclear, but passengers of a less adventurous nature were offered plainer fare as an alternative.

What's new?

What's new? For British Airways' business passengers in 1977 it was the new Club cabin on the 747 aircraft, which was extended to all UK–US routes from October 1978.

British Airways' 'Elizabethan' service menu cover gives it a medieval air, with an image of Queen Elizabeth I. Muhammad Ali, the famous boxer, after autographing one such menu, annotated it 'The Greatest', but we think that meant him and not the menu!

The Best of British

A hook to attract the important North American market has often taken a British heritage line, and a royal one at that. BOAC had the 'Monarch' brand for its one-class deluxe services and 'Majestic' and 'Coronet' for its two-class routes. In its early years, British Airways used a simple and traditional 'First Class', but in 1981 launched 'Crown First Class' as its new premier-product brand name worldwide. The main product feature was a 'sleeperette'-style seat that had been tested successfully in the summer of 1980 on the 747 routes to West Coast USA, the Far East, Australia and Africa. No one had offered such a product since the 1950s Boeing Stratocruiser pull-out bunks, but there the comparison ends. Up to twenty hours in a noisy, propeller-driven aircraft with two stops to refuel on the way could not compare to the luxury of seven hours' slumber in a non-stop 747.

On European routes, a completely different approach was taken, but both 'Crown First Class' and what came to be known as the 'New European Product' were adaptations of in-flight products designed to meet their respective markets' changing customer needs and expectations. Trialled successfully on London–Paris during 1980, then rolled out progressively across Europe, the old First Class and Economy products were removed entirely. Not 'Crown First Class' but 'Club' and 'Tourist' classes were introduced. There was little demand for a First Class service on most short-haul European routes, but certainly something in between was needed and Club fitted the bill. Broadly speaking, Club offered a fully flexible fare, increased baggage allowance, enhanced ground services and high-quality in-flight meals, snacks and complimentary drinks. Tourist customers benefited from the new Eurobudget fares and carry-on meals on the longer routes, a rather good deal given the early seating was exactly the same for both classes – the single-passenger cabin was divided merely by a moveable curtain dependent upon the size of the Club or Tourist loads.

In 1980, to emphasise their 'British' credentials, British Airways dropped 'airways' from its brand name. It was an old idea that had taken time to become acceptable. Negus & Negus, who had designed the original British Airways' livery, had always intended that the word should be removed within a very short time from the airline's main launch in 1974, but it had been a step too far for many. By 1980, however, British Airways was trying to find its way in a changing world that was becoming increasingly full of new British airlines. The single word 'British' was considered the best way to make British Airways stand out and to emphasise its national identity and pre-eminence. In the words of the Chief Executive, Roy Watts, 'In this one word, *British*, we express our own confidence that in this field, British is Best – and that we are the Best of British.' There was still a lot of hard work to do before that aspiration could be truly met.

Right and far right: Using the astral crown from its coat of arms, British Airways launched its new 'sleeperseat' as part of a 1981 relaunch of its First Class product, to be called 'Crown First Class'. As the advert says, 'Fly the British way for a new standard of excellence', a nice play on words linking back to a livery change that shortened the British Airways name on its aircraft to just 'British'.

Fly the British way
for a new standard of excellence

The British love to excel. We'd be the last to deny it. So when we looked for ways to enhance the traditional exellence of First Class service on our 747s, we knew we'd set ourselves a challenge.

Now we'd like your verdict on the result. We call it Crown First Class.

It starts where your journey begins – at the airport. Naturally, you have exclusive check-in desks and a quiet lounge away from the throng. At London's Heathrow airport

you share Concorde's prestigious check-in area. On board, the first thing you'll notice is spaciousness. If the seats look a little different, it's because they have the ability quickly to convert to superbly comfortable Sleeperseats. We had to leave a lot of room to make this possible, so you benefit from the extra space throughout your flight.

Lie back and relax. We'll introduce you to a standard of excellence that's wholly British.

British airways

CROWN
FIRST CLASS

British
airways

CROWN
FIRST
CLASS

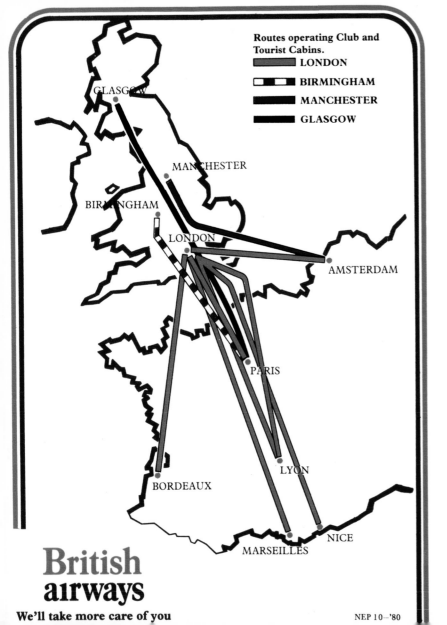

Routes operating Club and Tourist Cabins.

—— LONDON
—□—□— BIRMINGHAM
▬▬▬ MANCHESTER
▬▬▬ GLASGOW

GLASGOW

MANCHESTER

BIRMINGHAM

LONDON

AMSTERDAM

PARIS

BORDEAUX

LYON

NICE

MARSEILLES

British airways

We'll take more care of you

NEP 10—'80

Above and left: During late 1980 and progressively through 1981, new Club and Tourist products were rolled out across British Airways' European routes. By this time British Airways was beginning to rationalise what its key product features should be, but there was some way to go before the brand-name differentiation was removed between what appeared to be the same products.

The Survival Plan

The 'Crown First Class', 'Club' and 'New European Product' initiatives were just two examples of a range of product changes made by British Airways in the late 1970s and early 1980s to attract more traffic. The market was ever more challenging as the effects of US deregulation bit deeper and new entrants as well as established airlines came and went. There was serious overcapacity on most routes. While turnover had risen each year, from £647 million in 1974 to £1,640 million in 1978/79, margins were uncomfortably small. With a projected re-equipment programme cost of £950 million to replace 100 aircraft that would not meet new noise limitations by 1986, something more needed to be done. One approach was to centre the long-haul fleet on the 747 for the dense routes and on the similarly RB211-engined Lockheed TriStar 500, yet to be delivered, for the less dense routes. Short-haul would centre on the Lockheed TriStar-1 for the dense routes and two new aircraft, the Boeing 737 and Boeing 757, also yet to be delivered, to replace the Trident fleet on the European and UK domestic routes.

While all these changes were moves in the right direction, especially on product improvements, something more drastic had to be done. By 1980, while turnover increased again to £1,920 million and passenger numbers were up 10 per cent, profit hardly moved at £11 million. The company had too much debt and operating costs, mainly fuel, were up over 27 per cent; all this in the face of a deep economic recession that was beginning to take grip as the world worried about the effects of an impending conflict between Iran and Iraq. The UK government had already announced their intention to privatise British Airways, but it was clear that chipping away at the edges of its debt and cost burden would take many more years before the company could be in a sound financial shape for a successful flotation. This was unacceptable and a new Chairman, Sir John King (later Lord King of Wartnaby), was appointed with a reinvigorated board to oversee the path to privatisation. Sir John was not an airline man but a successful industrialist nicknamed 'Mrs Thatcher's favourite businessman'. If anyone could steer British Airways towards a successful flotation, he could.

The survival plan, as it became known, was drawn up during 1981 and saw unproductive routes cut and staff numbers substantially reduced. There were just too many staff for the slimmed-down airline, a legacy of the original integration seven years previously that had resisted all efforts to whittle numbers down. British Airways had earlier tried to improve employee productivity as one way to grow into its staff numbers, but the recession stopped that approach in its tracks. By 1982, staff numbers had been reduced by nearly 30 per cent over their 1979 peak, a reflection of the flexibility, imagination and willing co-operation at every level of the management, staff and trade unions.

Fleet replacement slowed, although retirements of older aircraft were accelerated. The first 747 freighter that was delivered in 1980 was quickly sold. As the recession deepened, several new 747-236 aircraft were delivered straight into storage and not into service. The key element of the restructuring plan, however, was to load the 1981/82 accounts with £426 million of extraordinary charges to reflect provisions for expected staff severance, increased write-down values of certain aircraft and disposal of other assets. The overall deficit for the year was £544 million, a substantial loss by any account but a necessary course to remove some of the burden of British Airways' inherited legacies. Without the survival plan and government financial guarantees for the airline's capital and debt reconstruction, severely but unfairly criticised by some at the time, British Airways may never have become 'the World's Favourite Airline'.

Above: The new Boeing 757 was a key part of British Airways' survival plan to operate on European and UK domestic routes, including shuttle services.

Left: Although British Airways had to make substantial cuts across its business as part of its survival plan, its focus on customer service was not lost. The very successful 'Club' concept was further enhanced in 1981 by a 'Super Club' service on UK–USA routes, a super standard to supersede old Club and again take it above the competition. The new 'Expanda' seats were wider than many airlines' first-class seats and at six-abreast on US routes were an industry leader, with a middle seat that converted to a table.

The World's Favourite Airline

The beneficial effects of the survival plan began to be seen as early as the following year. While widespread competition and overcapacity persisted, the deterioration in British Airways' finances was stopped. While the financial position remained serious, a major turnaround had been achieved, with costs considerably reduced, productivity dramatically improved and a net profit made of £77 million. While passenger numbers fell they were more than offset by reduced capacity and increased revenue, especially from the business passenger market. While customers were becoming more price-sensitive on many routes, especially the North Atlantic, they were responding to the new focus on customer service, punctuality improvements and new products. An improved Club product, Super Club, had been introduced on the UK–US routes during 1981 and European Club had become established as the new standard for business travel, with traffic up over 10 per cent during 1982. British Airways had every reason to face its future with greater confidence.

British Airways had started life as the airline with the world's largest route network. Capitalising on that strength in depth, by 1982 the company was carrying more passengers to more countries than any other airline and doing so as an airline of choice to many – it was a natural step to reflect that as 'the World's Favourite Airline'. British Airways' new advertising agency, Saatchi & Saatchi, came up with an imaginative plan to re-establish the airline in the market by emphasising its strengths, its recent improvements and its customer service. The campaign theme of 'the world's favourite' was widely acclaimed across the world and set the scene for British Airways' long haul back to profitability and the longer-term aim of a successful flotation.

Launched in 1983, British Airways' new advertising campaign was based on the theme of 'the World's Favourite Airline'. The campaign won immediate recognition for its striking technical and creative qualities and was certainly very different from anything that had been done before. It made the point that the new British Airways was going places. (Saatchi & Saatchi)

We fly more people to more countries than any other airline.

The world's favourite airline. British airways

The central premise of being the world's favourite airline was that British Airways flew more people to more countries than any other airline, a premise that became the central part of a series of striking images of faraway places overlaid with an aircraft silhouette. (Saatchi & Saatchi)

Putting the Customer First

Colin Marshall (later Lord Marshall of Knightsbridge) joined British Airways as Chief Executive in May 1983 and set about putting the customer first. Meeting the needs and expectations of customers became the dominant theme of Colin Marshall's early years. His background was in the competitive USA car hire industry and he fully appreciated the need for a clear and consistent customer focus, from first impressions through delivery to final destination. Importantly, were customers' expectations being met? In this regard, the airline business was no different from any other service industry; that message needed to be recognised and delivered with consistency and care if British Airways was to meet its corporate objective of being the best and most successful airline in the world.

'Putting People First' was the initial programme established for front-line staff to encourage a people-orientated working environment as the basis for focusing attention on the customer; in other words, learning how to work together more effectively. Similar programmes were established for support staff and, importantly, for managers. 'Managing People First' was aimed at all management levels, very much focusing on meeting British Airways' corporate objectives. Management now fully recognised that the future of the company depended upon a high standard of motivation and training if it was to succeed in an increasingly competitive world.

IN PURSUIT OF EXCELLENCE

BRITISH AIRWAYS

Above: 'In Pursuit of Excellence' was a summation of progress in achieving British Airways' focus on putting the customer first. Improving the quality of customer service was to become a way of life for all employees and would soon be enhanced by the launch of a new livery and a reinterpretation and re-emphasis of British Airways' coat of arms.

Right: Launched in 1982, the British Airways Executive Club was a further step toward the airline's goal of quality and excellence in all aspects of its service to customers. The original aim was to provide the best airline club in the world for frequent business travellers, but has since been extended to all frequent flyers.

Become a privileged member of this exclusive Club...

...and enjoy time and money saving facilities worldwide

Competition Policy, British Style

British Airways had long ago accepted that encouraging a competitive environment was to its advantage, at least in the UK. It had the size, experience and Heathrow in which to fight its corner if it was to meet the UK government's objective of a successful flotation by the mid-1980s. All to the good except that, while British Airways might have considered itself a first among equals, the UK Civil Aviation Authority took a more oblique approach. Although operating a competitive regulatory licensing system in which licences were held on merit but could be challenged by prospective new operators, this was not, in the CAA's view, quite enough to encourage a competitive UK aviation industry. In a 1984 policy consultation, the CAA recommended that British Airways should be reduced in size relative to other British airlines, that its lucrative routes to Saudi Arabia and Zimbabwe be transferred to British Caledonian (BCAL) and, to cap it all, that all its scheduled service licences from Gatwick and UK regional routes to Europe be given to other UK airlines. Heathrow slot frequencies would also be reduced to allow in new UK domestic trunk services. So much for competition.

Fortunately, the UK government took a more considered view, but it was still financially painful. The CAA's proposals were largely rejected in favour of encouraging more competition generally. Jeddah and Dhahran were transferred to BCAL and their South American routes transferred to British Airways (they had originally been taken from BOAC in the 1970s), hardly a fair swap and at an adverse cost to British Airways of £18 million per year. The CAA's riposte was to introduce a licensing system that encouraged competing licence applications even at the risk of some impairment to existing services. There would be no protection for existing licence holders whatsoever and an implied preferential leaning to new applications, with the interest of users also given increased prominence. In the new world order of UK route licensing, there clearly would be no presumptions in favour of existing licence holders. It was to be, if not quite a free-for-all, no quarter given or requested. British Airways' future focus would be on what was right for it as an airline, its customers and its future shareholders.

A Touch of Class

On 1 April 1984, British Airways took over all the rights and liabilities of the British Airways Board; in effect, British Airways became a UK traded company but with all its shares held by the UK government. It was a first formal step towards privatisation, which the airline hoped could come as early as 1986. British Airways had fought off the CAA's ill-judged attempts to weaken the company and establish a planned competitive UK airline industry and the bulk of British Airways' route network had been preserved. The continued focus on costs and customer service was also achieving results, with three consecutive years of substantial operating surpluses making British Airways one of the world's most profitable airlines by early 1985.

There was a renewed vigour in the company, with strong and effective staff support an integral part of the airline's new look and feel. This support for 'their' airline in opposing the CAA review had been particularly effective. A key part of the new look was the introduction of a new livery and uniform progressively introduced from December 1984. The British Airways coat of arms and motto, 'To Fly. To Serve', for the first time became a central part of the new contemporary livery design by Landor Associates. The design was considered to be 'a touch of class' and very appropriate for an airline not only reported to be 'the world's favourite airline' but rapidly building a reputation for quality and efficiency second to none.

There were clouds on the horizon, however, with two outstanding issues to settle before privatisation could proceed with the best chance of success; the UK and US governments had yet to finalise negotiations on a new air services agreement governing which airlines could fly between the two countries – the so-called Bermuda II Agreement – and there was also an outstanding antitrust lawsuit. Without a satisfactory conclusion to both these issues, prospective shareholders might consider that taking a financial stake was too risky. Privatisation was therefore delayed beyond 1986, much to the airline's disappointment.

Right: Where else indeed might BCAL have been flying to in the Middle East if the UK CAA had succeeded in its misguided attempt to cut British Airways down in size?

Far right: From Concorde to the BAC 1-11, all BA's fleet types in the new Landor livery.

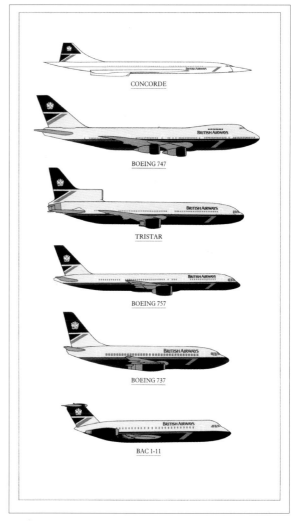

TAKING OFF...
A GREAT NEW STYLE

Above left: 4 December 1984: British Airways takes off with a great new corporate image. Keeping the old quarter Union Flag tail fin design, the aircraft were painted midnight blue with a pearl-grey top. What was new was the reinterpretation of British Airways' coat of arms as a more contemporary graphic, a new clarity of style placed centre stage on each aircraft's tail fin and elsewhere throughout British Airways. While there was still no explanation to observers of what the motto meant, its original purpose had long been clear. It had been proposed to the English College of Heralds in the early 1970s by British Airways, but rather kept under wraps. It was what the company did and why. Shortly, it would have both customers and shareholders to satisfy.

Above right: A 1989 pre-delivery test flight of two British Airways 747-400 aircraft, displaying the Landor livery to perfection.

Opposite left: A new livery complemented by a new uniform. Designed by the French couturier Roland Klein, British Airways' new uniform was stylish and of its time. The 'deckchair pattern', as it affectionately became known, was at once flattering and flattening. Drape shoulders and straight skirts suited some but not all, but that was the 1980s!

Opposite right: Earlier in 1984, British Airways extended its Super Club product across all long-haul routes worldwide. To emphasise the size of the new seats, promoted as 'the widest seat in the air', the launch ads 'lowered' the seats through the aircraft's roof. (Saatchi & Saatchi)

The widest seat in the air.

Our new Super Club business class offers you the widest seats in the air. So wide that they aren't the easiest to fit through the door. And so wide that there is only room to fit them in six abreast instead of the usual eight. But though the seats may be few and far between, the cabin attendants are not.

There are just as many of them as before, which means they can now give you more personal care and attention than ever.

So now Super Club is on all our long-haul routes, you'll find that however far you go your flight will be a calm and restful one.

British airways
The world's favourite airline.

Privatisation

The years from 1982 to 1987 had been a turning point for British Airways. As well as a record-breaking £3 billion turnover, capital debt had been reduced from over £1 billion to less than £300 million, with capital reserves built up to over £600 million. British Airways' profile could not have been higher.

Bermuda II negotiations had largely maintained the status quo on air traffic rights and the antitrust suit had been settled. The UK government therefore considered the time was right and announced that British Airways would be privatised early in 1987. The share offer closed on 6 February 1987 with a total of 720 million shares issued to 1.2 million investors on the London, New York and Toronto Stock Exchanges. So popular was the share offer that it was eleven times oversubscribed and the shares jumped 68 per cent on the first day of trading. Privatisation had at last given British Airways the opportunity to develop its business as it saw fit.

Freed from government control and the financial limitations of the UK Treasury, British Airways could focus on its commitment to customer service and becoming a leader in market innovation. As a quoted company, British Airways could now attract new external financing to augment its working capital and facilitate its business development. Despite its newfound freedom, however, British Airways still operated in a highly regulated commercial world. Most other major airlines remained under government control and protection and it would remain a competitive struggle for British Airways to achieve its objectives. This was completely understood and accepted. The issue was more about achieving a level playing field and a fair opportunity to compete.

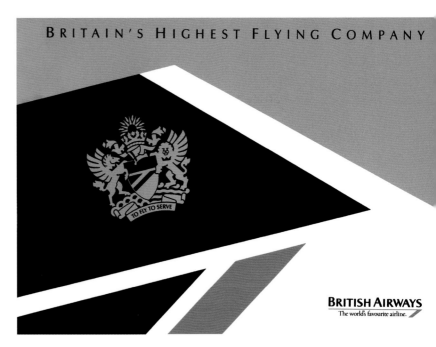

BRITAIN'S HIGHEST FLYING COMPANY

BRITISH AIRWAYS
The world's favourite airline.

'Britain's highest flying company': issued as part of the flotation as an explanatory document on British Airways, the public did not need a glossy brochure to know a good deal when they saw one. Eleven times oversubscribed, British Airways staff also piled in, with 94 per cent of them taking shares and a direct financial interest in the company's performance.

British Caledonian

By 1987, British Caledonian had become the major second force in British aviation. It operated to Africa, the USA, the Middle and Far East and throughout Europe and carried 2.5 million passengers a year. By any measure it was a significant medium-sized airline.

The middle ground was not the place to be, however. Without the economies of scale available to the larger airlines or the operational flexibility of the smaller, niche carriers, BCAL was squeezed in between. By early 1987 it was clear that this situation could not continue and that a solution would be to merge with British Airways. In July 1987, the proposed merger was announced but was then subject to a hotly contested takeover battle, with SAS looking to strengthen its international operation by constructing a European airline partnership. By December British Airways had improved its offer and the merger was approved.

The merger was too good an opportunity to miss to strengthen British Airways' position in the short- to medium-term future. By absorbing BCAL's fleet of 747s, Douglas DC10s and BAC 1-11s, British Airways also strengthened its position at Gatwick.

British Airways acquired some very valuable assets with BCAL: a skilled and dedicated workforce with a deservedly high reputation for service and a route network that meshed well with BA's own. The UK Monopolies and Mergers Commission accepted that the concept of BCAL as a second force airline had been rendered obsolete by the fundamental changes in the worldwide aviation industry since the early 1970s. The creation of an artificial, planned UK airline industry and the creation of an illusory competitive environment was not the way to go. What was needed was the genuine article and the merged airlines created just that.

The CAA, however, continued to attempt to interfere in the inevitable process of natural selection in the development of the UK airline industry. BCAL's Gatwick–Europe route licences were not handed to British Airways, instead being put out to competing bids from other UK airlines, but the competitive element ended there. Even where there was the opportunity to have two UK airlines licensed on the same route, British Airways' applications were refused. This was not in anyone's interests, particularly those of the consumer, as the opportunity for a competing service was denied.

BCAL was an impressive airline for its size but was caught between a rock and a hard place in the competitive dogfight that had taken over international air travel in the 1980s. With US deregulation providing an almost constant stream of new, thrusting entrant airlines and very low prices, the middle ground was not the place to be.

West & Central
Africa

British Caledonian
Airways

Above: BCAL's first-class service was a well-respected product in the 1980s.

Left: The West and Central African routes had been taken from BOAC and given to BCAL in 1971. They were profitable routes for BOAC, contributing some 3 per cent of its worldwide revenue; a considerable 'gift' to BCAL to provide artificial help to allow it to grow and take on the mantle of the UK's 'second force' airline.

British Caledonian Airways

TIMETABLE FIRST EDITION

Valid 18th March until 30th July 1979
Subject to alteration without notice

The 'Caledonian Girls', as BCAL's stewardesses became known, were an attractive sight in their Scottish clan tartan uniforms.

Gatwick

Heathrow has always been British Airways' main operating base since it opened in 1946 as the premier airport for London. Until the early 1950s it was the only airport for London of any note, with Croydon never regaining its pre-Second World War level of operations and finally closing in September 1959. In the early 1950s the UK government designated Gatwick to be the second London airport and the operational alternative to Heathrow in poor weather; nowhere else was considered geographically near enough to be a real London airport. With the massive rise in air travel during the later decades of the twentieth century, several contenders became established to a point in the 1980s where even places as far away as Luton and Southend started calling themselves a 'London' airport, much to the annoyance of Heathrow and Gatwick and the airlines that operated from them.

The old Gatwick Airport had closed in 1956 for a complete redevelopment and reopened in 1958. BEA quickly placed its Channel Islands operations there as a means of reducing the already growing pressure on Heathrow slots and terminal space. As Heathrow grew and space tightened further, both new and existing airlines started Gatwick operations. The growth of charters in the 1970s and 1980s also spurred growth at Gatwick. The UK government played its own part in effectively forcing some foreign scheduled airlines and the remaining Heathrow charters to Gatwick, except Concorde, in order to lessen Heathrow demand and delay restricting air movements. By the time the new Gatwick North Terminal opened in 1988 and became British Airways' Gatwick base, Gatwick had become the second-largest airport in the world in terms of international traffic. With the acquisition of BCAL Gatwick assumed a greater importance for British Airways, with over thirty flights a day operated. More would follow as British Airways tried to maximise the use of both Heathrow and Gatwick as part of a two-hub strategy for London with a redistribution of operations between the two airports. Later events would

force a rethink as the aviation world readjusted to the threat of terrorism and the continuing rise of the independent low-cost airlines in what remained of the twentieth century.

Gatwick's Martello Terminal Air Station, commonly known as 'The Beehive', was a key feature of the new Gatwick Airport opened in 1936. The UK Director-General of Civil Aviation, with some foresight, wrote in British Airways Ltd's Gatwick handbook, 'London's needs will inevitably demand in the future a ring of airports around its metropolis.' He also recognised the problems of delays in terminal capacity and the need for good ground communications and links such as railways with airports. A pity his words were not heeded by successive governments.

PRICE SIXPENCE   No. 4

BRITISH AIRWAYS

OFFICIAL HANDBOOK

TERMINAL HOUSE, 52 GROSVENOR GARDENS, LONDON, S.W.1

A British Airways Ltd Fokker F.XII about to depart from Gatwick's Martello Terminal in 1936. (Kenneth A. McDonough)

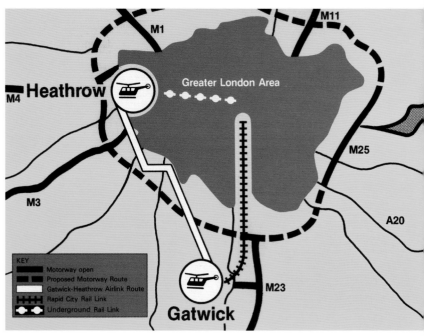

Above left: Reopened in 1958, the new Gatwick terminal and railway station look almost deserted, with just a few BEA aircraft in sight to confirm this is a new airport.

Above right and below left: Before the M25 was opened in 1986, moving passengers between Heathrow and Gatwick was a slow road journey or a long connection by rail and bus via London.

To make transfers easier and soften the controversy of forcing some foreign airlines to Gatwick, the UK ATLB licensed a helicopter shuttle in 1978. Operated jointly by BCAL and British Airways Helicopters using a British Airports Authority-owned Sikorsky S61, the ten-flights-a-day service at a one-way fare of £12 was itself controversial, liked by passengers but disliked by local residents along the route due to the helicopter's high noise levels.

British Airways' takeover of BCAL helped strengthen its position at Gatwick with additional slots, aircraft and route licences, although BCAL's European licences were taken away by the UK CAA.

The Challenge of the 1990s

The 1990s were predicted to be a decade of unparalleled growth and change for world aviation. The market had become global and growth was forecast to increase by 6 per cent per annum, a cumulative expansion of some 80 per cent by the end of the decade, doubling the size of the industry. British Airways' objective was to take advantage of this expansion and maintain its position as the world's leading airline, but it could not do this alone or by continuing to focus upon its traditional markets. Partnerships with other airlines would be needed at both ends of the size spectrum in order to offer an integrated system with consistent service throughout.

What had become clear by the end of the 1980s was that regulatory change was happening much faster and necessitated substantial changes to the way airlines would do business in future. The European Union had enacted its first Common Air Transport Policy in 1988, which would give wider traffic rights to EU-registered airlines. Further changes to apply EU competition laws and increased fare liberalisation were also anticipated. These moves toward a less closely controlled and protected industry were creating an environment of opportunism that encouraged the prediction of new growth.

British Airways' early attempts at partnerships involved successful transfer traffic relationships with American Airlines (AA) in the mid-1970s and United (UA) in the early 1980s, both huge US airlines. British Airways would have to match or make alliances with airlines such as these if it was to make deeper inroads into the huge US market. AA and UA, both with substantial domestic feeder services, had been nominated to replace the struggling Pan American and Trans World Airlines on UK/US routes and could not be ignored. The UA relationship changed to one with USAir before focusing solely on AA, marking the first examples of what came to be called 'globalism', a new strategic process that would see alliances of airlines wax and wane over the next decade as the process of integrating services and products worked its way through. Closer to home, a proposed

20 per cent equity share by British Airways in the then Belgian national airline, Sabena, in conjunction with KLM, failed to achieve EU regulatory approval. The idea was to establish a new airline, Sabena World Airlines, using Brussels as a hub, to serve seventy-five European cities, but it was as yet a step too far in these fledgling days of EU regulatory change.

What was worrying, however, was the UK's blunt attempt at further liberalisation. Allowing more airlines into Heathrow, particularly US airlines, subject to slot availability, was one thing, but bringing about the transfer of four of British Airways' slots at Tokyo's Narita Airport and giving them to Virgin smacked of the old days of attempts at planned competition.

An early attempt to widen opportunities to access the US market was a joint initiative between British Airways and American Airlines in October 1975 to interline over US gateway points.

Space travellers
The new Club Europe cabin

Join us in the new Club Europe cabin. We've launched our widest ever seat for Club Europe passengers and redesigned the cabin's interior exclusively for business travellers. The surroundings are welcoming and the new cabin divider offers greater privacy.

Above: 'We have lift off', the introductory theme to introduce British Airways' new Club Europe. The airline's biggest-ever investment in European travel, Club Europe provided a clear differentiation between the old Club and Tourist brands with an improved cabin divider and wider seats.

Left: A precursor to the deeper alliances of the 1990s was British Airways' 1987 marketing joint venture with United Airlines. A programme of co-ordinated ticketing, schedules and baggage handling effectively opened a small gateway to the 150 US cities served by United, with reciprocal use of one another's terminals in New York, Washington and Seattle. The venture went some way to smoothing transfer traffic and increasing passenger numbers for both airlines, but was only a skirmish in the truly global battle to come for the major key markets.

Naming the Brands

As well as new partnerships, British Airways continued its focus on customer service. The company had a long record of winning awards for its airline service and by the early 1990s these were differentiated by brand to give an encouraging insight into customers' perceptions of British Airways' products.

In the previous decade British Airways had become the world's first airline to adopt a policy of branding its individual classes of service to ensure each had a distinctive place in the air travel market. This approach was designed to create a brand promise – an expectation about the product and service that passengers could rely on – and to ensure the consistency and competitiveness of each brand offering.

Club had become the world-standard businessman's preference, which in 1988 was further differentiated into the Club World and Club Europe brands. The World Traveller and Euro Traveller brands followed in 1991, designed to provide a more relaxed approach to on-board service to meet the tastes of the 1990s. The old 'Crown First Class' product was initially renamed, improved and relaunched as a 'First' brand in 1995, but what was missing was a linking element, a core identity around which all the brands would revolve and relate to, in essence a master brand, which the name 'British Airways' would itself become. As the master brand, 'British Airways' was the ultimate brand promise.

Winning awards is usually preceded, and hopefully succeeded, by good results. In the 1990/91 financial year British Airways carried 25.6 million scheduled and charter passengers, including 19 million internationally, which maintained the company's performance as the world's largest international airline, carrying more international scheduled passengers than any other. Just as BEA had advertised itself in the 1960s as the Number 1 in Europe, British Airways rightly saw itself as leading in the global airline business and maintaining its assertion to be 'the World's Favourite Airline'.

Above: Euro Traveller was the replacement for the old European routes' Tourist class. On long-haul routes, World Traveller similarly replaced Tourist. At last, British Airways had a clear-cut range of product branding: First on all long-haul routes; Club World and Club Europe; World Traveller and Euro Traveller.

Opposite: An attractive in-flight menu for one of British Airways' new World Traveller services to the Middle East, which includes a small quiz. (Maggie Kneen)

Illustration by Maggie Kneen.

WHERE IN THE WORLD?

This picture contains clues that will reveal a British Airways World Traveller destination.

Can you identify the destination?

Can you spot all 10 clues?

For the answer, see inside this menu.

BRITISH AIRWAYS

BA 6775

World **Traveller**

The World's Biggest Offer

Recession and the First Gulf War halted the lofty predictions for a decade of growth almost from the very start. The year 1990 had started well, with an 11 per cent increase in British Airways' passenger traffic over the previous year, but the Iraqi invasion of Kuwait stopped that growth in its tracks and traffic fell by almost a third virtually overnight. It was no consolation that British Airways fared much better than its competitors and there was also a much closer, almost personal, element in that one of the company's 747 aircraft was caught on the ground as the fighting erupted and was lost; fortunately there were no casualties but the aircraft's crew and passengers were held hostage for some months before being released.

The Gulf conflict could not have been predicted and its effect was dramatic; it demonstrated the fragility of an industry dependent upon free trade and personal freedom of choice to travel. While the US market was very badly affected by the fallout from the Chernobyl nuclear power incident in 1986, this time the effect was worldwide. A 'Go for It America' campaign had encouraged the US market back following Chernobyl, but this time it would need something much bigger.

British Airways took a proactive approach to promote and market its way out of the recession. 'The World's Biggest Offer' campaign was launched to give away on 23 April 1991 every seat across the British Airways' network. The intention was simple: to give British Airways' business a powerful kick-start. Coupled with its new brand offerings and the attraction of new, longer-range aircraft such as the 747-400, British Airways' business gradually came back and experienced faster growth than its major competitors as markets recovered; the year ended with a reasonable profit, greatly helped by British Airways' ability to act swiftly to contain its costs with a range of cost efficiency programmes, not least in facilitating flexible staff working.

Looking ahead, the expectation remained for continuing growth across all markets despite the risks of cyclical and unexpected events. What would be the real future limitation, however, would be the lack of infrastructure to cope with, let alone properly manage, the predicted growth in passengers, freight and overall air movements. Many of the world's airports were nearly full in terms of runway slots or terminal capacity – both, in the case of Heathrow; because of these limitations, British Airways had to look further afield if it was to continue to expand. Developing new regional services was one option, with a hub-and-spoke operation to be developed at the new passenger terminal Eurohub, being built at Birmingham. Manchester, Birmingham and Glasgow would become British Airways' three regional UK hubs both for European and long-haul operations.

The long-awaited decision to begin planning for Heathrow Terminal 5, intended to house all British Airways' operations by the early 2000s, would not be made for several years, but the signs were promising. As ever with UK airport planning decisions, it was a long, drawn-out process to the point where Heathrow's position as the premier world airport began to be seriously threatened as European airport competitors in Amsterdam and Paris rapidly grew larger.

Opposite top left: The world's biggest temptation: the contest to win a free seat on Concorde, or even any free seat would do, was such an understandable success that it kick-started British Airways' recovery out of the recession of the early 1990s.

Opposite right: Schiphol Airport in Amsterdam has long been a major competitor for UK long-haul passengers. With little Dutch originating traffic of its own, KLM has leveraged the size and facilities at Schiphol for many years to encourage business via its home airport. Many smaller regional UK airlines took advantage of this, flying passengers direct to Schiphol that otherwise might have gone to Heathrow or Gatwick.

Opposite bottom left: British Airways' new advertising campaign, called 'Global', was launched worldwide in early 1990 and became an instant hit, winning several major awards. An endearing use of hundreds of people in coloured costumes creating happy faces, it was intended to communicate the caring and friendly characteristics of British Airways' staff and emphasise the size of the airline's network. (Saatchi & Saatchi)

Changing planes at Schiphol

August 1991

Amsterdam Airport Schiphol

Engineering the Future

British Airways entered the 1990s with one of the largest and most modern aircraft fleets in the world. The re-equipment programme to replace the ageing aircraft inherited at British Airways' formation nearly twenty years earlier was by now well advanced. Twenty-one new aircraft had entered the fleet in the 1989/90 financial year alone, including two new types, the 747-400 and Boeing 767-300. Nineteen more aircraft were due the following year, including another eleven 747-400s, bringing the 747 fleet, already the second-largest in the world, to more than fifty. The Rolls-Royce RB211 engine family continued as the engine of choice for British Airways' larger aircraft, already powering the 747-200 and Lockheed TriStars.

Taking delivery of so many new aircraft presented an unparalleled challenge to British Airways' Engineering and Flight Operations departments; nearly a third of the engineering workforce and around a quarter of the pilots needed to be retrained. Total Quality Management (TQM) was at the same time introduced throughout Engineering, making a major contribution to improving reliability and punctuality as part of British Airways' objective to ensure its aircraft were the safest and most reliable in the world. Engineering was soon to go much further in refining its engineering facilities. Taking advantage of Welsh Development aid grants, new engineering facilities were to be opened at Cardiff Airport and in the Welsh Valleys. British Airways Maintenance Cardiff (BAMC), Avionics and Interiors Engineering would rapidly set new standards in cost control and maintenance practices that would make the department second to none in engineering British Airways' future.

First Delivery
British Airways 747-400
July 26, 1989

The first two 747-400 aircraft line up nose-to-nose for a promotional shot at Boeing's Seattle factory prior to delivery. The longer-range 747-400s were able to serve Tokyo non-stop and Australia with one stop.

Above left: A Boeing 757 undergoes major overhaul at British Airways' Heathrow engineering base. From the planks of wood and chains used in the 1920s to every modern facility, British Airways Engineering has travelled a very long and proud road, leading the UK and world aviation in the highest standards of skill and expertise over ninety years.

Above right: BAMC's £70 million maintenance base at Cardiff-Wales Airport was opened in June 1993.

Globalisation

The recurring theme of the early/mid-1990s was the move towards a global, open economy, simply defined as an accelerated integration and interweaving of national economies through trade, investment and capital. Commercial aviation could not fail to be part of that.

As part of the continuing trend towards further deregulation, the USA was now pioneering an 'open skies' approach to the control of air services between the USA and Europe to allow unrestricted access by each country's airlines. Unsurprisingly, the Dutch national carrier, KLM, was keen to promote 'open skies' as it had far more to gain from access to the vast US market than the US airlines would have from the Dutch. Others were opposed or somewhere in between. British Airways was keen to exploit the opportunities, but even the world's favourite airline had its limitations. The early deal with American Airlines was giving more strength in depth across the Atlantic through an ability to offer a wider range of products and services, but moves within Europe itself were now anticipated. British Airways believed that Europe's airlines would, within the next decade, be part of only three or four amalgamated European groupings with smaller, regional airlines serving niche markets. It was a telling foresight of the shape of things to come, but the path of aviation 'globalisation' would not run smoothly or consistently.

Europe at last began to offer new opportunities following years of prevarication. The European Union introduced the Single European Market (SEM) in 1993, in theory allowing any EU airline to operate air services between any two member countries and limited 'domestic' services within any EU country. Theory and practice can often be different, however, but the SEM did encourage British Airways and others to spread their wings. The creation of the German airline Deutsche BA by several German banks, with British Airways taking a minority shareholding, allowed re-entry to German domestic air services that only the year before had seen the closure of British Airways Internal German Services following the reunification of Germany. The purchase of a major shareholding in the French airline TAT European Airlines in 1992 and investments in Air Liberté during 1996 were two further opportunities that were viewed suspiciously by some, unhappy to see a non-French company involved with the offering of air services in their own backyard.

British Airways' first major step in its globalisation policy was taken in 1992 with a conditional agreement to invest up to US$750 million in USAir, the then third-largest domestic airline in the USA, and associated commercial agreements covering code sharing on USAir domestic flights, joint sales efforts and frequent-flyer programmes. This was a substantial deal which was predicated on integrating progressively as far as possible the operations of the two companies. It would have brought access to the huge North American domestic market, some 40 per cent of all world air travel, but failed due to US attempts to impose unacceptable conditions. A revised deal the following year for a smaller equity percentage did pass the regulators and became a successful operation, increasing US domestic feed to British Airways services to 42 per cent of its total US carrier feed. Although the USAir commercial agreements were ended four years later following British Airways' announcement of a broader alliance with American Airlines, the investment was a groundbreaking precursor to much deeper and stronger global alliances, which would follow within a few years.

Deregulation was at risk, however, of becoming that in name only, the removal of one set of rules on entry to new airline services merely being substituted with rules limiting what the successful existing airlines could do; all largely due to various governments' own failures to provide sufficient airport and air traffic control infrastructure to allow air services to develop naturally to meet growing demand.

Right: The forerunner of the **one**world alliance that was formed in 1998 was the formation in 1993 of what was believed to be the world's first global alliance, between British Airways, USAir, Qantas, TAT and Deutsche BA. It was the natural follow-up to the investments British Airways had made only months earlier in these airlines and was British Airways' direct response to the opportunities presented by deregulation, which it believed, all things being equal, would allow the development of a single global market in air transport. What the alliance offered was the global reach of its partner airlines into all four corners of the world. It was truly a 'service' partnership that prospectively offered major benefits to customers and the airlines themselves. It would take several years to develop and partner airlines would come and go, not least USAir as its fortunes faltered, but it would be the model upon which the **one**world alliance would base itself.

Far right: An early Deutsche BA timetable cover.

British Airways' charter subsidiary Caledonian Airways was sold in 1995 to Inspirations plc. The last manifestation of British Caledonian, it fell victim to the refocusing of British Airways' business to core services and the belief that future success as a charter airline would best be achieved by vertical integration with a successful tour operator.

The introduction of British Airways' World Images livery was such a new and radical concept in the airline's identity that it needed some explanation: 'See it. Feel it. Ease into it. And please, be part of it.' It was clear this would take some getting used to, and for many people the tail fins never did.

A Twenty-First-Century Airline

The last years of the 1990s saw British Airways pushing the aviation envelope yet again. Not content to sit on its laurels as the world's undisputed leading airline, it was looking to create and present itself as a new company for the new millennium, an approach seeking to continue to anticipate changing travel trends and responding to them. British Airways believed that its customers were looking for a more open, cosmopolitan style of service from an airline that was more global and caring. Times were changing and British Airways believed it had to change to reflect that and become a truly twenty-first-century airline.

A new identity was considered a key element in clearly expressing British Airways' new purpose in an inspirational way. It was to express the idea of British Airways as a 'citizen of the world', an airline of and for the world representing British Airways' global reach and service to the myriad of world communities. The concept of world citizenship was given a visual form in a highly distinctive manner: a series of artworks from around the world called 'World Images' that were painted on the tail fins of all British Airways aircraft and incorporated into other elements of the company's identity.

Painters, sculptors, ceramicists, weavers, quilters, calligraphers and paper artists from around the world were invited to produce an 'uplifting celebration' of their own community. Fifteen works were initially commissioned, with more to follow. Some designs never made it beyond the proposal stage and were consigned to the archives. Those that survived were striking and diverse, classic examples of their style and beautifully represented. Launched in 1997, the new livery was presented as British Airways' commitment to a more cosmopolitan approach to its service and products, which themselves were to receive a range of enhancements.

The 'World Images' livery, as it became known, was an intentional break from traditional corporate branding based on uniformity, consistency and control, but while the main elements of the British Airways master brand were also changed, they maintained their consistency in a new and refreshed format. The old 'Speedwing' red flash evolved into the 'Speedmarque' red-and-blue ribbon, complemented by a new typeface and palette of British Airways' red, white and blue corporate colours.

The designs were as much controversial as they were admired; they drew compliments from abroad but criticism at home. The loss of the representation of the UK's Union Flag drew particular dissent, except where it was shown on Concorde. Concorde's livery had remained all-white – it had to be to cope with the high temperatures operating at Mach 2 speeds – but its tail fin was a flowing depiction of the Union Flag designed by the Admiral's Dockyard Flag Loft in Chatham Historic Dockyard, Kent. It was itself a World Image and a British one at that. Together with the new British Airways master brand elements, the Union Flag design was subsequently adopted across the British Airways fleet to become the new livery for the twenty-first century. The concept of World Images was of its time, but events moved them rapidly on.

Above left: As part of the drive to define what it saw as twenty-first-century air travel, British Airways launched a £600 million package of new products in January 2000. The most significant was a new Club World cabin with seats that converted to fully flat beds, the first in the industry, and followed the provision of flat beds as part of the new First brand re-launch in 1995. The new Club World cabin changed forever the way business travellers flew and was a major success, clearly setting British Airways apart from the competition.

Above right: In October 2000, British Airways introduced World Traveller Plus on selected routes. Many business passengers travelled in World Traveller but wanted more comfort at a more affordable price. World Traveller Plus was the answer, with its own cabin, extra legroom and extra baggage, a service now available on all long-haul routes worldwide.

Left: The Union Flag tail fin and the 'Speedmarque' logo became the elements that made up the new British Airways master brand for the twenty-first century.

Oneworld ... Revolves Around You

In 1990, there were 172 alliances of one form or another; by 1994 there were 300, and by 1999 around 500. Four were 'global', in the sense of a developing worldwide network; apart from the British Airways/USAir alliance, KLM and Northwest started the ball rolling in 1989, followed by the Atlantic Excellence Alliance of Delta, Swissair, Sabena and Austrian Airlines and the Star Alliance of United Airlines, Lufthansa, Air Canada, Thai Airways International and Scandinavian Airlines System. None except the Star Alliance stood the test of time in their original format, but they demonstrated that in order to compete effectively it was the way to go.

In 1998, the **one**world alliance was announced. The results of British Airways' deepening relationship with American Airlines had clearly shown the benefits of forging marketing alliances with real depth and strength, as had the Qantas relationship flowing from the Joint Services Agreement. The **one**world alliance initially joined together British Airways, American Airlines, Canadian Airlines, Cathay Pacific and Qantas into a global affiliation, which included code sharing, frequent-flyer programmes, the sharing of airport lounges and the promise of a seamless travel experience for alliance customers to around 600 destinations in 138 countries. In 1999, Finnair and Iberia joined, with LAN Chile and Aer Lingus following. Both British Airways and American Airlines took shareholdings in Iberia as part of Iberia's privatisation programme, a clear indication of the value of Iberia to the alliance and future business opportunities in the South American market, where Iberia had strong air service links and traffic flows.

By the late 1990s, British Airways had forged not only a global alliance in **one**world, but was also benefiting from close links with small feeder airlines under a new concept of franchised services, an increasingly important element of British Airways' global links. Started in 1993, franchisee airlines were liveried in British Airways' colours and this concept would provide almost 50 per cent of British Airways' feeder traffic by 1995. By 1999, there would be five franchisee airlines at Gatwick alone: City Flyer Express, Brymon, British Regional Airlines, BASE and GB Airways, with Air Liberté and Deutsche BA as endorsed partner airlines operating in their own liveries. More would follow. The shape of the aviation industry had changed to reflect both the opportunities and challenges of the 1990s, but as it entered the twenty-first century there would be ever greater and deeper commercial, operational and structural challenges to face.

By 2013, the **one**world alliance had grown to twelve full members, with twenty-two affiliated members and three members elect, including USAirways following its merger with American Airlines.

LONDON-GATWICK / PARIS-ORLY

Champagne

air Liberté

Above: A British Airways 747 and American Airlines 767 line up at Heathrow.

Left: Air Liberté's Gatwick–Orly advertising.

Hard Times

The turn of the millennium was not the best of times for British Airways. The challenges of the industry since privatisation were taking their toll and some business opportunities had not met expectations. A serious currency crisis in Asia and excess capacity on the North Atlantic had also impacted results.

The first loss since privatisation was announced in early 2000 and further measures were put in place to add to the stripping of £1 billion in costs from the business that had begun in the late 1990s. Further bad news was to follow. The tragic loss of an Air France Concorde grounded the Concorde fleet, and it would be another fifteen months before the aircraft returned to service.

Undaunted, British Airways began the long haul back to profitability only to be hit by probably the worst day in aviation history. The terrorist attack on the World Trade Centre in New York on 11 September 2001 caused chaos across the aviation world. British Airways was particularly badly hit as it operated to many US destinations. Aircraft were grounded, flights slashed and 7,000 jobs terminated. While services resumed quickly, the effects on future operations would be severe and enduring.

Top: Following the terrorist attack on the World Trade Centre in New York, all US domestic and international flights to and from the USA were grounded for several days. Services resumed but with enhanced security measures that caused serious delays and still reverberate around the operation of all air services worldwide.

Bottom: Concorde's return to service with Alpha Foxtrot on 7 November 2001 was considered a welcome and symbolic sign of the recovery and rebuilding of New York City following the 9/11 attack. 'Welcome back, Concorde,' said New York's Mayor Rudolph Giuliani.

Future Size and Shape

In February 2002, British Airways unveiled a major package of measures designed to return the company to profitability. Known as Future Size and Shape, the package sought to achieve a 10 per cent operating margin from £650 million annualised cost savings, including further job losses and a drastic restructuring of the short-haul business to meet the challenge of the 'no-frills' airlines.

The message from Rod Eddington, the Chief Executive, was simple: 'We will remain true to our heritage of being a full-service network carrier, committed to customer service excellence and world-class products but we must transform British Airways into a simpler, leaner, more focused airline so we can thrive and prosper in an increasingly competitive market.'

By 2003, British Airways' fleet was reduced and simplified, building on earlier fleet rationalisation measures that included substituting 747 orders for the smaller and more versatile 777. Overall, capacity was reduced by 21 per cent and at Gatwick by 60 per cent.

Future Size and Shape was an almost total restructuring of British Airways' business model and a change in company culture. It was British Airways' survival plan for the twenty-first century and another milestone in British Airways' history. The major difference from the survival plan of the early 1980s was that no one was going to ride to British Airways' rescue, which the UK government effectively did back then by underwriting its balance sheet. This time the company was on its own and could only rely on itself and the continuing support of its shareholders.

The smaller and more versatile Boeing 777 would become a central part of British Airways' modified fleet as part of the Future Size and Shape package. With Gatwick capacity reduced by 60 per cent, its operations would centre on Boeing 737s and 777s only.

Above left: Ten years later, British Airways would open a new chapter at Gatwick by moving into a new, state-of-the-art facility at Gatwick North Terminal. Gatwick had become the UK's second-largest airport and the base for many of British Airways' long-haul leisure routes and European and domestic services.

Above right and below: An important part of Future Size and Shape was a close and continuing focus on customer service and making British Airways stand out from the competition. In 2006, an improved Club World cabin was introduced with wider and more comfortable flat-bed seats. With elegant interiors and softer lighting, the new Club World was a perfect invitation to a good night's sleep, almost like being at home. (*Below:* MCSaatchi)

Club World. More beds, more places, more often. **BRITISH AIRWAYS**

Full Service, Low Cost

A critical part of the Future Size and Shape package was changing British Airways' short-haul business model. Making short-haul profitable had always been a challenge, but with the rise of the 'no-frills' airlines it was becoming even more difficult.

A particular problem was the complexity and variety of British Airways' UK regional operations. Since the late 1980s, several UK independent airlines had merged into British Airways: Dan Air followed BCAL, with Brymon, City Flyer, British Regional and Manx at various intervals. Each brought added complexity in fleet size, aircraft types and operating bases. British Airways had also created its own low-cost airline, GO, but the experiment had not been successful and GO had been sold. Things had to change.

The formation of British Airways CitiExpress in March 2002 began the transformation. It merged four of British Airways' regional airlines into one to offer a new, low-fare, regional product, giving greater choice and flexibility. A major advertising campaign was also launched on international routes based on the promise of full service at 'no-frills' prices. With fares as low as £69 on Paris and Amsterdam, the response was encouraging and the results promising. Pre-tax profits were up and major cost savings achieved. There could be no going back.

Top: British Airways CitiExpress was itself renamed BA Connect in February 2006 as the need to reduce costs further with a revised product offering became necessary. In November 2006, BA Connect was sold to Flybe, with only a few key routes, such as those from London City, being retained. British Airways also retained a 15 per cent shareholding in the business and the RJ 100 aircraft for its London City UK domestic and European services.

Bottom: GO lines up with the competition, somewhere in Europe.

Above: There were no pots of gold at the end of the rainbow but the 777 would provide much-needed flexibility and cost benefits under the Future Size and Shape plan.

Right: Full service at 'no-frills' prices became a centrepiece of British Airways' fight to more than match the low-cost airlines. (Bartle Bogle Hegarty)

€59 one way
Book at ba.com
LONDON
BEGINS
WITH
BRITISH
AIRWAYS

Concorde returned to service in 2001 but had suffered badly from the serious reduction in business traffic following the 11 September attack. Her retirement in October 2003 saw the end of the commercial supersonic era. It was a sad farewell but the time machine had reached its final destination. Six British Airways Concordes now grace museums in the UK and abroad and the seventh remains at Heathrow. Alpha Foxtrot resides at Filton near Bristol, here seen passing over Brunel's iconic suspension bridge in a salute to nineteenth- and twentieth-century technological innovation. (*Above:* South West News Service)

The final landing

Heathrow airport 24th Oct 2003

The French Connection

'Open skies' is the name of the agreement between the USA and EU that allows any airline from those countries to operate air services between them. It is the current manifestation of aviation deregulation that started in the USA in 1974, then in the EU in 1987 and slowly beyond that. It is definitely not a complete open house for any US or EU airline to fly anywhere and join in with anyone; even US deregulation does not go that far. While the US promotes competition, it does like to control it where it suits, not least on entry to its domestic market, although things are also gradually changing there as **one**world and the other global alliances continue to develop.

OpenSkies is also the name of the British Airways subsidiary 'that combines French chic and *savoir-faire* with an all-American can-do attitude across the Atlantic'. It is definitely not another manifestation of TAT or Air Liberté, the former British Airways subsidiary investments from the 1990s, which were part of British Airways' first global alliance. Those airlines faltered and were eventually sold in the face of fierce competition from Air France and others unable to accept a non-French controlling interest in their territory.

OpenSkies is different. Now part of **one**world, OpenSkies is among the first of a new breed of what's called 'boutique' airlines, low-cost but with class and customer service on a par with the best. Operating from Paris's Orly Airport to New York's JFK Airport and Newark's Liberty International Airport, its fortunes have fluctuated since its formation five years ago, but largely due to the world economic downturn and not regulatory or competitor interference. It represents the changed face of what was once a totally commercially regulated aviation industry. It may be a niche player, but it is an important part of the **one**world alliance and its global reach.

4

ALL TOGETHER NOW

The first decade of the twenty-first century was a long haul back to recovery from the appalling events of 11 September 2001, compounded by the banking crisis and world economic downturn in the following years. Those years saw both achievements and some disappointments for British Airways, but overall there were signs of real progress. The effects of 11 September had forced an intense review of the path ahead. Activities that were no longer appropriate or necessary were gone. A close and constant control of costs and a clear and focused perception of the future allowed British Airways to edge towards recovery by the end of the decade. However, while British Airways believed it could continue to be successful as an independent airline within a global alliance, there was a risk the company might not achieve the full value that was possible as part of a stronger organisation with greater scope and opportunities. Ten years before, British Airways had been the second-largest European airline in revenue terms, but it had slipped back by 2010. It was not necessarily about overall size, but overall value in revenue growth terms and standards of customer service; in other words, not the biggest but the best.

In April 2010, British Airways and Iberia signed a formal merger agreement that came into effect on 24 January 2011. The merged company was to be called the International Airlines Group, S.A. (IAG), with the British Airways and Iberia brands continuing to operate separately as two subsidiaries under the IAG group umbrella. Nearly forty years earlier, British Airways was the new name in aviation; now it was IAG.

The new company would serve 200 destinations with over 400 aircraft, with expected total annual synergies of €400 million after five years. In fact, the merger offered much more than that. It represented the new face of aviation in the twenty-first century, maintaining the best of both airlines' brands and services across their combined route networks. The merger further strengthened the **one**world alliance, but left open the opportunity to consolidate with other airlines over time. With the possibility of further liberalisation on US and EU routes, there remained the distinct prospect of further airline consolidation both within the USA and within Europe and even between the airlines of both areas. IAG would be well placed to take advantage of that.

Three years into IAG's formation, it has not all been plain sailing. As ever, the global economy remains the arbiter of the fortunes of the airline industry, with rising fuel prices its major cost. The effect of the banking crisis of 2007/08 and resultant world economic downturn continues to drag at many countries' economies, not least Spain's, but things are slowly beginning to improve. Total expected synergies by 2015 have been increased to €560 million, enhanced by the addition of Vueling Airlines into the IAG family in 2013 and increasing revenues; a new North America–Europe joint business agreement between British Airways, Iberia and American Airlines delivered US$8 billion in 2011, significantly ahead of expectations. All together, the IAG airlines are the new name in aviation.

Above left and middle: British Airways' report to shareholders in November 2010 filled in the missing piece in British Airways' globalisation jigsaw.

Above right: Despite the global downturn, British Airways continued to deliver on its promise as official sponsor of the British Olympic team for the Beijing Olympic and Paralympic Games in 2008. The amazing results from Team GB were just a springboard to the even greater triumphs to come at the London 2012 Games. (Bartle Bogle Hegarty)

Concorde's flight numbers BA001 and BA003 were reintroduced for the inauguration of the first London to New York services out of London City Airport. Using an Airbus A318 aircraft with a thirty-two-seat, all-business configuration, the flight refuels in Shannon, where US customs and immigration clearances are completed, allowing customers to depart quickly on arrival in New York. (Nick Morrish)

British Airways: 'To Fly. To Serve.'

British Airways' contribution to IAG during the past three years has been strong and growing. Pre-merger losses had approached £1 billion, faster than costs could be cut, global demand had slumped and fuel prices continued to rise. Urgent action was needed to shore up a depleted balance sheet, including a refocus on customer service and brand expectations and delaying deliveries of new aircraft. By late 2010, demand for air travel began to pick up again and the long-awaited Terminal 5, which had opened in 2008, was proving the promise it offered when it was first envisaged over twenty-two years ago. Building on that promise, in September 2011 British Airways launched a new manifesto, reinterpreting its coat of arms and reinforcing its motto, 'To Fly. To Serve.' These four words were themselves a promise. A promise and expectation at the heart of everything the company did and everything the company is. As a start, British Airways committed to investing more than £5 billion up to 2016 in new aircraft, smarter cabins, elegant lounges and new technologies to make its customers' travel experiences more comfortable in the air and on the ground.

The year 2012 was a particularly good year for British Airways. Revenue from its airline partnerships was growing strongly and there was a perceived passion and belief in the British Airways brand throughout the company. That passion was enhanced in April with the acquisition and integration of bmi into British Airways, strengthening significantly its position at Heathrow. Shortly after began the long-awaited London 2012 Olympic and Paralympic Games, where British Airways was the official airline partner, which lifted both the company and the UK economy generally. British Airways' Olympic sponsorship campaign was a great success and gave a profound boost to the company's fortunes.

The year 2013 has maintained British Airways' promise and customer expectations. Two major new aircraft types, the Boeing 787-8 'Dreamliner' and Airbus A380, entered the British Airways' fleet, the first new aircraft types for seventeen years. From order to delivery it took six years – longer than anticipated and, rather like buses, the two arrived almost at the same time, on 27 and 30 June 2013 respectively. The logistics of fleet acceptance, integration and operation were complex and of a scale possibly never experienced before at British Airways. That this was successfully accomplished says much for the skill of British Airways' people, from its engineers and pilots to planners and marketeers and many others, a continuation of a long tradition of quality, innovation, service excellence and pride in a job well done.

British Airways has travelled many millions of miles since becoming the new name in aviation in 1974. It has done everything expected of it in those last forty years, building on its rich heritage, expertise and innate ability to innovate and move forward. It is now indisputably one of the world's most prestigious and trusted airlines, offering excellent service, a wide range of products and an extensive route network. There should be no doubt that it will continue to lead into the next century.

'To Fly. To Serve.' British Airways' reinterpreted coat of arms and motto makes the perfect medal stamp as the proud airline partner for the London 2012 Olympic and Paralympic Games. '2012. We're ready' says it all. (Bartle Bogle Hegarty)

Terminal 5 has rapidly proved the promise it offered when it was first envisaged over twenty-two years ago. Now considered one of the best airport terminals in the world, it begins the journey on British Airways. It marks that journey as something special, something effortless and exciting, something memorable. Something to do again. From Heathrow's 'tent city' in 1946 to Terminal 5 in 2014, British Airways' customer experience on the ground has come a very long way. (Nick Morrish)

Above: British Airways' 2012 advertising also included a very successful 'Don't Fly' campaign to encourage visitors to the London 2012 Olympic and Paralympic Games. (Bartle Bogle Hegarty)

Right: The British Airways 'Firefly' aircraft brings the Olympic flame from Athens to RNAS Culdrose, ahead of the Olympic torch relay. The flame was carried in a ceremonial lantern, similar to a miners' 'Davy' lamp, which was fitted in a specially designed cradle, firmly fixed to its aircraft seat using a secure holding device. The aircraft also carried special guests HRH The Princess Royal, Lord Coe, David Beckham and the Mayor of London. (Nick Morrish)

Above left: The British Airways Airbus A319 aircraft painted in the 'Firefly' livery and carrying the logo of the London 2012 Olympic and Paralympic Games. (Nick Morrish)

Above right: In the run-up to the London 2012 Olympic and Paralympic Games, British Airways worked with Turner Prize-nominated artist Tracey Emin to mentor a British talent to create an aircraft livery. As a result, a number of British Airways aircraft were decorated as 'Doves' as part of this project. (Geoff Lee for British Airways)

Left: bmi had effectively become the new 'second force' UK airline following the takeover of British Caledonian, but it too suffered BCAL's fate of being in the middle ground. Too grown-up to be a niche-market player and too financially weak (despite the backing of Lufthansa) to compete with the major airlines, bmi did not survive the global downturn of 2007–2010. Purchased from Lufthansa in 2012, bmi's assets were merged into British Airways; their Heathrow slots were particularly valuable acquisitions and allowed British Airways to continue to develop its route structure despite Heathrow's severe runway capacity restraints.

Above left: British Airways' 2013 advertising campaign heralded the arrival of the A380 aircraft. With 469 seats over two decks with six cabins, the aircraft presented another challenge in both operational and engineering terms. Quieter and with lower cabin pressurisation, greater humidity and mood lighting, the customer experience has taken a further step upwards. For the interior designers, it is space, space and more space and a perfect setting for their creative talents to deliver something original, something distinctive and unmistakably British Airways – an experience that customers expect from one of the world's leading global premium airlines. (Bartle Bogle Hegarty)

Above right and below right: The Boeing 787-8 Dreamliner is something else again, technologically ultra-modern in its construction, mainly of composite materials, and with twenty-first-century styling for the aircraft's interior.

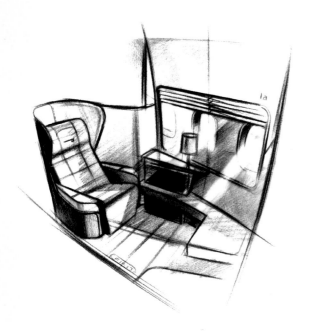

British Airways' long experience – together with its predecessors' nearly a century of journeys – means it is in a stronger position than others to shape the future of flying. From flying boats to flat beds, it's what makes the company different. FIRST defines that difference, a new level of style, service and comfort second to none. Welcome to British Airways. (forpeople)

EXPERTISE

RICH HERITAGE

EXCELLENT SERVICE